...my a' Detroiter!
XOXO —
Karen

I'm Keeping

My Money

I'M KEEPING

MY MONEY

Using God's Principles to Achieve Financial Security

Jerome D. Gibson

iUniverse, Inc.
New York Lincoln Shanghai

I'm Keeping My Money
Using God's Principles to Achieve Financial Security

Copyright © 2007 by Jerome D. Gibson

iUniverse books may be ordered through booksellers or by contacting:

iUniverse
2021 Pine Lake Road, Suite 100
Lincoln, NE 68512
www.iuniverse.com
1-800-Authors (1-800-288-4677)

Because of the dynamic nature of the Internet, any Web addresses or links contained in this book may have changed since publication and may no longer be valid.

ISBN: 978-0-595-42387-3 (pbk)
ISBN: 978-0-595-86723-3 (ebk)

Printed in the United States of America

The information, ideas, and suggestions in this book are not intended to render professional advice. Before following any suggestions contained in this book, you should consult your personal accountant or other financial advisor. Neither the author nor the publisher shall be liable or responsible for any loss or damage allegedly arising as a consequence of your use or application of any information or suggestions in this book.

This book is dedicated to God, my wife, my mother, my family, and my teachers. All have stuck by me through the good and bad times.

Also, to all the mothers who didn't want their children to follow the crowd.

It's no fun being a broke adult.

—Jerome Gibson

Contents

Introduction
God's Help

In 2003, I watched friends, fellow church members, and neighbors suffer when the dot-com boom died and the stock market fell, taking their jobs with it. These events opened my eyes to what was going on around me. Every day, I heard people complain about their lack of money and the fact they couldn't make ends meet. These were not people who lived on the street, but people whom I grew up admiring because they had the latest of everything: cars, clothes, jewelry, and plenty of cash. However, when things started changing in our economy, these individuals didn't have a clue what to do when they lost their jobs or received massive pay cuts.

It was a surreal experience seeing these formerly well-off people worry about where their next meal was coming from, whether they were going to lose their home, and how bleak the future looked for them. This could not have come at a worse time as prices shot up and salaries were eliminated or greatly reduced. The jobs they relied on failed them miserably.

It was then, after getting married, that I realized that these individuals had squandered their golden opportunity to carve out a life for themselves that could have withstood a job layoff or a massive salary reduction. I didn't want to end up like them, because I realized that the few good years they had living it up didn't compare to the lifestyle they presently found themselves forced to live in. I wanted a better way of life for my new family, so I decided not to follow in the footsteps of people who were now struggling. I wanted to start things off on a different route, because if you do what you know will result in failure, you are a fool. I'm about to take you through the process that has allowed me to keep the money that I so diligently worked for, and you can follow this same process so that you don't throw money away.

So, praise the Lord! We are about to embark on a journey to help you become the wise steward that the Lord wants you to be. We should realize that the resources we have are not ours. They are a blessing from the Lord, and he has made us a steward (manager) over his resources. Before we get started, let us pray:

Father, in the name of Jesus, I ask that you bless me to receive the wisdom to better manage the resources that you have provided. Also, Lord, I ask that you will allow your will to guide my life. I ask all these things in your precious son's name. In Jesus' name, Amen.

There are a few key passages from the King James Version of the Holy Bible that will help to set the groundwork for this book. We want the Lord to bless us, so we must follow his way of doing things. Just as when we were children, we knew there was a right and wrong way to ask for things from our parents, now we are about to learn the right way to ask for things from God. With our prayers, we adhere to the Lord's admonition.

"And he spake a parable unto them to this end, that men ought always to pray, and not to faint." (Luke 18:1)
"Therefore I say unto you, what things soever ye desire, when ye pray, believe that ye receive them, and ye shall have them." (Mark 11:24)

Let me clarify what I believe this last scripture means; it means if you ask for things that are according to his will, he will do them as stated here:

"And this is the confidence that we have in him, that if we ask anything according to his will he heareth us." (1 John 5:14)

In combination with a sensible budget, a plan for retirement, and mastering basic financial concepts such as saving and avoiding debt, you can follow the methods I've outlined in the next chapters to achieve a life of financial comfort.

"God is not a man, that he should lie; neither the son of man, that he should repent; hath he said, and shall he not do it? Or hath he spoken, and shall he not make it good?" (Numbers 23:19)

If your will is the Lord's will, you will achieve any goal you desire in your life because he must keep his word. Therefore, we are ready to begin, and I hope and pray that you will receive this as the Lord sees fit.

1

Call to Responsibility

Does your cash always seem to dribble through your fingers? Have you ever wondered why as soon as you think you're ahead, you keep finding yourself short before the end of the month? Maybe you're making more money than you've ever made. Maybe you once told yourself, "When I make forty thousand a year, I'll be okay." But then it becomes fifty thousand a year, and you still come up short. Do some of these sayings ever pop into your head:

- I just need a million dollars, and I'll be all right.

- I'll always have debt.

- The more I make, the more I'll spend.

- I can't take it with me.

- If I just made a little more, I would live more comfortably.

These are common statements that most of us have heard in one way or another, and deep down inside, we may carry out day after day. Think about it: prices have continued to rise over the past five to ten years; the goods you could buy for $100 in 1997 will now cost you nearly $129 in 2007 (Consumer Price Index 2007). And yet it still doesn't explain the attitudes—some are listed above—that many of us have embraced when it comes to saving money on items we need.

For instance, we all know that every week in the newspaper there are coupons that will save us money on food, hygiene products, dish detergent, laundry detergent, pet care, health and beauty items, and much more. But some people still refuse to buy the newspaper and clip the coupons. They use common excuses of not having time and not wanting coupons to dictate what they buy. My favorite excuse comes from deep inside: what would others think if they saw us always using coupons? Sometimes it is amazing and sad when people who are struggling financially put what others think above the welfare of themselves and their families. It's sad because the people whose opinions that they are worried about are not helping them pay any bills.

Remember Momma Said Don't Follow the Crowd

It is time to set aside these old attitudes and behaviors that have stopped your progress. You must rid yourself of the fear of not being accepted by those who are around you. Perhaps your mother warned you about following the crowd when it is in error. Did she ever say, "If everyone else jumped off the bridge, would you?" That saying may bring back memories, but it is evident today. You may see people living paycheck to paycheck, working two jobs, and complaining that they do not make enough money. Yet you may do the same things: paying top dollar for clothes, shoes, food, cars, vacations, movies, and the like. Therefore, you are jumping off the bridge with everyone else just to be part of the crowd.

If the majority of people you know were handling their money correctly, would you hear, see, or just plain know that they are going through these rough financial situations? You have to consider what you are doing with your money and whether you are doing it according to God's will.

"Now therefore thus saith the Lord of hosts; consider your ways. Ye have sown much, and bring little; ye eat, but ye have not enough; ye drink, but ye are not filled with drink; ye clothe you, but there is none warm;

and he that earneth wages to put it into a bag of holes. Thus saith the Lord of hosts; consider your ways." (Haggai 1:5–7)

If you're not getting the results that you'd like to get from your money management, then you know there is something that you're not doing correctly. Furthermore, I'm sure you've seen people who should be retired but are still working. They are working at fast-food restaurants, dry cleaners, grocery stores, and other companies that offer low-wage jobs that were once considered teenage jobs. A 2005 study by the Vanguard Group found that 35 percent of respondents who left full-time work in their sixties continued working due to financial necessity (Ameriks 2007). You can avoid this if you consider your ways and take better care of managing your money.

Managing your money means understanding general financial health by doing the following:

• Setting and keeping a budget

• Understanding your cash flow

• Making your purchases based on needs instead of wants

• Planning ahead for big purchases and retirement

• Saving your cash through discounting as described in this book

Some purchases are just downright foolish. Some people allow what everyone else is buying to determine what they should or should not have. Maybe you go to work and know that others are struggling just as you are, but your colleague pulls up in a new car, and all of a sudden, your older car that is paid off doesn't suit you anymore. You ask how they can afford it, but you cannot. Then as you drive home, you see many people with the latest cars, and you start to become dissatisfied with the car you presently have.

You start to believe that you need to buy a new car because you deserve it—and what is the point of working if you cannot enjoy your money? When one minor thing goes wrong with your older car, your mind becomes a steel trap, and nothing will stop you from getting a new car because now you have the greatest excuse of all: safety.

I will acknowledge that new cars have more safety features than many older cars; however, things can go wrong with new cars as well. Even when you go to get a new car serviced at the dealership—an oil change, for example—they check to see if there are any recalls on the vehicle and proceed to fix it. In essence, you can end up being inconvenienced waiting for the repairs to the recalled items on your vehicle. This could also include charges for renting a vehicle if your car needs to be held for a long period.

Moreover, when a new car breaks down for whatever reason, you must do the same thing you would with an old car: wait for a tow truck. Now, some of you will say, "With a new car, my warranty will cover it breaking down." Nevertheless, you have shifted from what you said was justification for you buying the car in the first place: safety. If you have to wait on the road for both vehicles, where is the safety? Why pay more for a new vehicle that potentially could put you in the same situation as your older vehicle? The same sort of logic applies to items such as stereos, television equipment, and clothing. It pays to question your own motives. When does a desire for a fancier television or the vanity of wanting new clothes become a problem? Think about it.

What Happens When You Are Irresponsible

According to Edmunds.com, a respected consumer car site, the average monthly car payment is $447, and loan terms average sixty-three months (Fallon 2003). If you finance your vehicle, then you're required to carry full-coverage insurance. According to the National Association of Insurance Commissioners (NAIC), the national average for insurance in 2004 was $838 a year for all cars (NAIC 2006). New car insurance is more expensive than insurance for used vehicles. Car insurance is based on your individual state's liability insurance, so there are extreme variations in costs. For example, in New York, the average for every insured driver that carries liability coverage is $1,171 annually, partly due to some of the high-density urban areas in the state. In contrast, drivers in

North Dakota, with fewer urban areas and lower subsequent risk, average only $562 a year for insurance.

Combined with maintenance costs, interest charges, and fuel, the total for driving a new car can easily top 25 percent of your gross monthly salary using the take-home pay of $2,000 a month. Even new cars have maintenance costs, and fuel expenses vary, of course, depending on your car's fuel efficiency, how much you drive, and what region of the country you're in. So it pays to add up the figures before you sign on the dotted line.

You may think that you need a new car when your old one breaks down. Most people do not get a full repair job done to their older vehicle, only patchwork, so your car is destined to break down. Let's say it costs $3,000 to get your car repaired, and you say that it is not worth putting all that money into your car when you can get a new one. Therefore, you go to get a new car even though you do not have good credit. You put down about $500 to $1,000, your monthly car payment is $453, and your full-coverage insurance, which you must get on a new car that has been financed, is about another $70 (more in some urban areas). You're looking at going through the $3,000 it would have taken to repair the old car in about six months, and then you operate at a loss from there on out.

Today, the average consumer borrows $21,000 at a 7.5 percent interest rate to finance a new car (Fallon 2003). If you assume your monthly payment is $453, then the total loan for 63 months equals $28,539. That amount doesn't include insurance. Even if you had to pay $3,000 a year to repair your older car, you would have saved over $13,000 after 63 months by not getting a new car.

Here's an example, showing the monthly costs of buying a new car versus keeping your paid-off used car (assuming $3,000 a year repair on the older vehicle):

New Car vs. Paid-Off Used Car

Item	New Car	Used Car	Savings (monthly)
Payment	$453	$0	$453

New Car vs. Paid-Off Used Car (Continued)

Insurance	$100	$70*	$30
Gasoline	$100	$100	0
Maintenance	$50	$250**	<$200>
Totals	$703	$420	$283

*Insurance may be lower because some coverage, such as collision and comprehensive, can be dropped.
**Maintenance costs rise as cars age.

Consequently, the ripple effect of living paycheck to paycheck will make you have to find other ways to generate more money to cover this new expense. You may have to work a second job or continue to run up your credit cards to make ends meet. If you have a family, you will put an unnecessary strain on your family in the name of keeping up with the Joneses. Precious time and resources, which could be used on your family, will be used up on a car that will be out of style in about a year or two when the body style is changed. Therefore, I ask you again, "If everyone else jumps off the bridge, would you?"

Debunking the Leased Car Myth

You may decide to lease a car instead of buying a new car. This is the worst thing you can do. The best thing you can do is keep your old car. The second best action is to buy a slightly used car. Buying a new car would be the third best thing. Your last choice should be to lease a car. This is because when leasing, you pay a lot of money to rent a car for two to three years. Leased car payments are the residual value of the vehicle spread over the term of your lease. You are paying the dealer the difference in what the car is valued at now versus what it will be valued at the end of your lease term, plus any interest and fees. Put simply, if the car today is worth $13,000 and in three years it is worth $9,000, you pay the $4,000 difference with interest and fees.

For example, let's say you find a car you want to lease, and you bring in a down payment of $1,500. Your monthly payments will be $350, and your insurance will cost about the same as buying a new car. In essence, the argument that I made against buying a new car is the same for a leased car. You will squander a lot of money while you are trying to control your spending. You will spend about $100 less a month leasing, but is it really $100 less? First, you will not own the car when your lease period is up. In addition, many people go over their mileage allowance, so you may pay an additional $0.12 to $0.23 a mile. If you, for example, drive an additional ten thousand miles, you will pay at least an additional $1,200. The table illustrates the difference between purchasing and leasing a new car.

Purchased vs. Leased Car

Item	Purchased Car ($21000)	Leased Car (Based on two year lease)	Cost Difference
Payment	$453	$350	$103
Insurance	$100	$100	$0
Gasoline	$100	$100	$0
Maintenance	$50	$50	$0
Mileage at $0.12/mile going over leased miles by 10,000 miles as monthly cost	$0	$50	<$50>
Totals	$703	$650	$53

The person that is leasing a car will only average about $50 less than buying a car. Now, the monthly lease payments will never stop for the person leasing a car, whereas the person buying a car will at least not have a car payment when their car loan is paid off. And it is amazing what people will do in order to continue leasing cars when buying a car is the better overall value. I've observed people with leased cars trying to use others for a ride so they can save their precious miles. Others will buy an older car to keep down the mileage on the leased vehicle. There are also fees for any damage to the leased car and other fees associated with the end of the lease. The car companies will gladly roll all these fees into another leased vehicle, so you will never stop paying them. Sounds like bondage to me. Remember, car companies are in business to make a profit, so don't you think when they allow the consumer to lease a car they are getting the better deal and not you? They are playing on your keeping up with the Joneses mentality to always have a new car. Again, I ask, "If everyone else jumps off the bridge, would you?" Now do not think I am opposed to you getting what you like, but I just want you to wait until you have taken control of your spending and can afford it.

Beware of the Crabs in Your Life

Being responsible is not a popular way of life, but it is necessary for those of us who want to get the most out of this life. We must go against the popular way of doing things and do what we know deep down is correct. Being an adult has little to do with age, but more to do with making the hard decisions that many young, unskilled people are not able to make. I am not going to tell you that this is going to be easy and that everyone is going to support you when you start changing your spending habits. You will get opposition from family, friends, coworkers, and others who will get upset with you for changing your way of life, because this will cast a reflection of themselves and what they need to do. Most people cannot handle looking at themselves and admitting that they are wrong. Therefore, they will act like crabs in a barrel, trying to pull you back in with them. They will do this, because when you become successful and responsible with your money, they will feel regret and embarrassment that they are stuck in a rut. It is to their benefit to drag you down with them.

If Uncle Mike teases you for driving a scruffy, but paid-off car, you can politely remind him that you don't have to make monthly payments. If a coworker makes fun of you about being careful where you shop for gas, it should be no skin off your back. The coworker isn't paying your gasoline bill every month. You can tell her that you live the way that suits you and your family's needs.

God's will, as stated in his word, is:

"If any of you lack wisdom, let him ask of God, that giveth to all men liberally, and upbraideth not; and it shall be given him." (James 1:5)

Here are some things to think about as you start this journey off the bridge:

- Have you bought into any of the money myths discussed in the introduction? Can you see yourself stepping away from those erroneous beliefs for the good of your budget and your family?

- Do you have a true picture of your current finances?

- Have you developed a monthly budget?

- Do you know your exact income and expenses?

- Can you distinguish between needs and wants for your purchases?

- Do you consider the purpose of your purchases instead of engaging in mindless spending or trying to "keep up with the Joneses"?

- Are you able to handle peer pressure, and can you let go of the need to follow the crowd?

- Are you willing to analyze purchases before you make them to compare costs?

2

What Is a Discount?

A discount by definition is a reduction made from a regular or list price. It is a price that is lower than the going rate on goods and services we need. You are trying to save money on things you need and not to accumulate all you can. There are situations where one believes that they have saved money, but they have not. Remember, when you buy something you do not need, no matter how inexpensive, it is not a discount.

There are three types of discounters that you want to avoid becoming: the over buyer, the unnecessary discounter, and the unwise discounter. Let's take a look at these.

The Overbuying Discounter

Consider Jonathan: his local grocery store normally has hamburger for $1.59 per pound, and he usually buys five pounds a week. This Saturday, his store had the hamburger on sale for $0.99 per pound, so he decided to buy ten pounds instead of five. Unfortunately, he actually spent $1.95 more than he had planned. Unless he's very careful about storing that extra hamburger properly, it may spoil, and he won't have saved anything at all. Imagine if this turned out to be a storewide sale and Jonathan did the same thing on twenty items. He would have gone over his weekly budget, overcrowded his kitchen, and spoiled his food. The result will be little to no savings.

Take a look at Amber. She set aside $50 to buy a pair of much-needed shoes, but when she got to the store, there was a sale on the shoes that she wanted for $20. Instead of keeping the $30 discount she would have received, she justified buying another pair of shoes and leaving with a $10 savings. If this occurs just three times in a year, she's spent $60 buying unnecessary extra shoes. This explains why there are so many unworn shoes in people's closets. Please don't play that stupid game of wearing the second pair of shoes once to justify getting them.

If you combine the first and second examples, you are missing $120 for items you more than likely will not regularly use. The key point to remember is it's not a savings if you buy an item you won't use.

The Unnecessary Discounter

Unnecessary discounters are those people who go out and buy items that they weren't even thinking of purchasing until they saw them advertised. Case in point: Anthony runs into the local electronics store to get a few blank DVDs. There he sees a big billboard stating that for a limited time, a fifty-five-inch television will be on sale for $1,999 instead of $2,999. He doesn't want to miss out on saving $1,000. But he should ask himself whether he is really saving. The answer is no, of course. If he was in the market for a television, he would not just be buying blank DVDs to record on a nonfunctioning television; he would have been shopping for a television. Instead, he spent $1,999 in order to save $1,000.

I would have kept the $1,999. Let the store save someone else $1,000 for an unnecessary item. There may be some of you with a perfectly functioning computer, but when you see a computer for sale, you'll justify buying it because it is marked down from $699 to $299. It appears you are saving $400, but just as in the television example, you "saved" $400 on a computer that you did not need. All it cost you was $299.

The Unwise Discounter

The unwise discounter is probably just as dangerous as the other two discounters. This person buys what they need, but does it in an unwise manner, wasting more than what they save.

For example, Angela leaves home with the express purpose of buying gasoline for her car. The first gas station charges $2.30 a gallon, so she keeps driving to find cheaper gas. She passes up four gas stations until she sees a gas station charging $2.28 a gallon. By driving four miles to get a $0.02 a gallon savings, she has spent more than she saved. A person must be wise not to travel long distances for little or no savings.

Let's take this previous example and make it a wise discount. Say you were going to see your grandmother, and you knew there were gas stations on the way. You saw that the gas was at $2.30 a gallon at the nearest station, so you continue to drive to Grandma's and come across a gas station that is charging $2.28 a gallon. It would then make sense to get the $0.02 a gallon savings because you are not going out of your way to get it. You have not wasted any more gas than what you would have if you stopped at the first gas station. In essence, I am telling you not to make an extra effort to save less than what you will lose. With that, gear up, focus, and because we are about to embark on this journey together, let's start discounting.

"Wisdom is the principal thing; therefore get wisdom; and with all thy getting get understanding." (Proverbs 4:7)

Things to think about:

- Are you willing to take a look at your spending patterns and develop new ways to manage your cash flow?

- Are you willing to examine your current spending patterns and make changes in order to receive discounts?

- Can you resist "sale" items when they are things that you don't need?

- Can you learn to distinguish between a genuine bargain sale price and one that is artificially inflated with no real savings?

3

The Non-Aggressive Discounter

For many of you, trying out my suggestions will be your first encounter getting a discount on various items. Let's start off by giving you some non-aggressive ways of discounting. *Non-aggressive* means that you do not have to spend much time and effort to gain significant savings. In this section, there will be no mention of clipping coupons, reading sales papers, or the other things most people dread doing. Those activities are for more aggressive discounters.

Both aggressive and non-aggressive discounters will benefit from this section. For the aggressive discounter, this will be another method of discounting to add to various other methods. For the non-aggressive discounter, these methods will allow you to save considerable amounts of money. You may feel that you're too busy to spend a lot of time trying to save money. You would rather go into a store, get what you want, and continue in your everyday lives. This section addresses the needs of those who feel they do not have the time to be an aggressive discounter.

Grocery Store Spending

Managing your grocery bill will have an immediate and positive impact on your cash flow. Everyone eats and shops for food, so taking control of your spending in the grocery store is a step off the bridge to financial ruin.

According to a United States Department of Agriculture (USDA), cost of food study published in February 2007, the average household of four spends $158.70 weekly on groceries (for a "low-cost" plan), which ends up being $634.80 a month (USDA 2007). If your take-home pay is $2,000 a month, that amounts to over 30 percent spent on groceries alone. This is troubling because this figure is based on food alone and does not include toiletries or other items needed to maintain your family's monthly needs. Of course, there are those of you that spend a little more or a little less, but the bottom line is you are probably spending too much of your income on groceries when there are easy and effective ways of keeping your money. One of these ways is using store loyalty cards.

Loyalty Cards

You may have heard of the discount cards given out at grocery stores, pharmacies, athletic stores, and other retailers. Nearly 86 percent of American shoppers use at least one loyalty card, according to a Boston University poll published in 2004 (Bosworth 2005). This means that you probably have used a loyalty card before. Many supermarkets and drugstores use these cards to collect information about their shoppers and to provide discounts to them as well.

These cards allow you to participate in the weekly and monthly savings that the store may advertise. These cards are like having a ready-made coupon in your wallet or on your key chain. There have been many days when I have been at the grocery store and noticed many people who did not have these cards and missed many savings. This is one of the easiest ways to save money without much effort. Initially, you'll have to ask about the card, fill out an application, and put the card in your wallet or on your key chain. But after that, remembering to hand the card to the cashier is the extent of your effort, and often the cashiers help you to save by asking, "Do you have your loyalty card today?" Signing up for the card is usually free.

In my personal experience, using these cards has saved me up to 50 percent on items that I already buy. If you have family members that shop, make sure that everyone gets a card. If you forget to use these loyalty cards, you may be cheating yourself out of a lot of money.

For example, I went to Kroger, which offers a loyalty card, and did a price comparison of a few commonly purchased products. Every week there is a different sale, so I randomly picked a particular week, August 7 to August 13, 2006, to compare the savings between regular and loyalty card prices.

To make this interesting, I used national brand products and not off-brand or store-brand products, except for the ground chuck, milk, grapes, and peaches, which didn't have a corresponding national brand, or, as in the case of the milk, people tend to buy the store brand anyway because it is usually cheaper. Additionally, I noted instances where the card didn't provide savings. This is what I found:

Canned/Bottled Foods	Regular Price	Loyalty Card Price	Savings
Mushrooms	$1.59	$1.00	$0.59
Peas	$0.75	$0.65	$0.10
Green beans	$0.95	$0.50	$0.45
Corn	$0.95	$0.50	$0.45
Baked beans	$1.69	$1.69	$0
Pineapples	$1.52	$1.52	$0
Spaghetti sauce	$2.69	$2.00	$0.69
Soup	$0.89	$0.89	$0
Total	$11.03	$8.75	$2.28

Snacks	Regular Price	Loyalty Card Price	Savings
Granola bars	$3.56	$2.00	$1.56
Crackers	$2.19	$1.00	$1.19
Cupcakes	$3.69	$2.50	$1.19
Peanut butter	$2.99	$1.99	$1.00

Strawberry jam	$4.49	$3.99	$0.50
Grape jam	$3.49	$2.99	$0.50
Total	$20.41	$14.47	$5.94

Cereal/Grains	Regular Price	Loyalty Card Price	Savings
Spaghetti	$1.29	$0.50	$0.79
Cereal	$3.49	$2.50	$0.99
Bread	$1.29	$1.00	$0.29
Hotdog buns	$1.29	$1.00	$0.29
Hamburger buns	$1.29	$1.00	$0.29
Macaroni	$1.39	$1.00	$0.39
Bagels	$1.89	$1.50	$0.39
Pop Tarts	$1.99	$1.99	$0
Rice	$4.49	$4.49	$0
Total	$18.41	$14.98	$3.43

Meat/Seafood	Regular Price	Loyalty Card Price	Savings
Ham (lb.)	$4.98	$3.98	$1.00
Chicken breast (lb.)	$5.29	$2.65	$2.64
Chicken wings (lb.)	$2.49	$1.25	$1.24
Drumsticks (lb.)	$1.79	$0.90	$0.89
Hamburger (lb.)	$1.78	$1.78	$0
Fish (lb.)	$9.33	$8.66	$0.67
Roast beef (lb.)	$4.99	$4.99	$0
Total	$30.65	$24.21	$6.44

Produce	Regular Price	Loyalty Card Price	Savings
Potatoes (5 lb.)	$3.99	$3.99	$0
Apples (3 lb.)	$3.29	$3.29	$0
Pears (lb.)	$1.79	$1.79	$0
Grapes (lb.)	$1.99	$1.99	$0
Bananas (lb.)	$0.49	$0.49	$0
Lettuce (head)	$0.99	$0.99	$0
Tomatoes (lb.)	$1.99	$0.99	$1.00
Cucumbers	$0.89	$0.50	$0.39
Strawberries (lb.)	$2.99	$2.00	$0.99
Celery	$1.79	$1.79	$0
Onions (lb.)	$0.99	$0.99	$0
Carrots (lb.)	$1.99	$1.99	$0
Total	$23.18	$20.80	$2.38

Beverages	Regular Price	Loyalty Card Price	Savings
Soda pop (two liter)	$1.59	$1.34	$0.25
Water (case)	$9.99	$5.49	$4.50
Orange juice (gal.)	$3.59	$1.99	$1.60
Lemonade (gal.)	$3.39	$1.19	$2.20
Fruit punch (gal.)	$3.98	$2.00	$1.98
Total	$22.54	$12.01	$10.53

Dairy	Regular Price	Loyalty Card Price	Savings
Eggs (doz.)	$1.25	$1.25	$0
Milk (gal.)	$3.29	$1.99	$1.30

Cheese	$2.69	$1.50	$1.19
Yogurt	$0.89	$0.50	$0.39
Margarine	$1.79	$1.00	$0.79
Butter (lb.)	$3.65	$3.65	$0
Cream cheese	$3.99	$3.59	$0.40
Ice cream	$5.29	$3.34	$1.95
Biscuits	$1.26	$1.26	$0
Total	$24.10	$18.08	$6.02
Grand Total	**$150.32**	**$113.30**	**$37.02**

The difference in price on this particular week is over 24 percent. Now let's look at what we did to get these savings: took less than two minutes to fill out a free application, put the loyalty card on our key chain, and let the cashier swipe the card. This is an easy process, but many people still do not bother to get the card to get all of these savings.

For example, the same day I went to Kroger, a gentleman in front of the line was asked by the cashier if he wanted to use another customer's loyalty card. The customer agreed, and when his total was complete, he saved a little over $6, a little less than 20 percent of his bill. He thanked the customer for the use of the loyalty card, but he didn't ask how to receive a loyalty card of his own. After the cashier swiped my card, I asked if many people didn't have a loyalty card. The cashier said that many people don't have the loyalty card, even though it would save them a lot of money. However, there are some consumers that have legitimate points as to why they choose not to get a loyalty card. Many people do not like the idea that a store can keep up with their identity and purchases. So, if you are one of these people and still want the loyalty card savings, there are some stores that provide their cashiers with cards to use in case a customer for whatever reason does not have a loyalty card.

If your grocery bill was the national average for a four-person household of $634.80 and you had a loyalty card that saved you 24 percent of what you normally pay, the savings would be $152.35 a month, or about 7 percent of your monthly take-home pay of $2000. Imagine what saving this extra amount of money would be over a three-year period. You would save $5,484.60.

The savings could be more dramatic if your household grocery expenses are larger. Even if you live alone, having a loyalty card will save you money on many of the staples you'll buy anyway.

For the average family of four, every year without a loyalty card might cost them $1,739.04. This is equivalent to or more than some people's monthly take-home pay. Are you getting excited? I know I am, because I am not doing anything extra for my trips to the grocery store except letting the cashier swipe my card, which takes seconds, and I am saving close to a month's salary per year.

Other Store Loyalty Cards

Loyalty cards are not just restricted to grocery stores; video rental stores, music stores, clothing stores, bookstores, pharmacies, and office suppliers often offer them to shoppers.

For example, there are athletic stores that provide loyalty cards for additional savings on shoes and apparel. Some of these athletic apparel stores will give you a $10 coupon just for signing up for the card. Unlike grocery store loyalty cards, your savings are mailed to you in the form of a coupon. Stores like Footlocker, Champs, Lady Footlocker, and Kid's Footlocker will send you a $10 coupon for every $50 you spend. This coupon can be used the next time you make a $50 purchase.

If you think about this, you could be buying these items anyway, so why not get $10 off your next $50 purchase? Let us look at this situation: Michelle buys her three children athletic sneakers that cost a total of $180. She gets her card swiped, and in a few weeks, she receives three $10 coupons. A few months pass, and Michelle has to buy more athletic sneakers for her children. This time, instead of spending $180, she buys the shoes separately to get $10 off each pair of shoes that are $50 or more and ends up paying $150 instead of $180. She saved almost 17 percent of what she was going to pay anyway. Also, she will receive more coupons for $10 because she spent over $50. So on top of her savings, she will get even more savings for using her loyalty card.

Come on, Get the Card

Now that we have established the worth of these discount cards, it is time to take action and get the cards. Each time you go shopping without a loyalty card, you are cheating yourself. For many of you, this may be your primary way to save considerable amounts of money, so you must take that first step to help enhance your savings by going to the store, filling out the application, and putting the card on your key chain. Also, there is nothing wrong with getting a loyalty card from multiple grocery stores, pharmacies, athletic stores, and other retailers, because the main idea is to save as much money as you possibly can. (The Reader Resources section has a partial listing of some retailers who offer this program.) So, get the loyalty card, and let's start discounting!

"But without faith it is impossible to please him: for he that cometh to God must believe that he is, and that he is a rewarder of them that diligently seek him." (Hebrews 11:6)

Things to think about:

- Can you take a few minutes to fill out the paperwork at stores where you regularly shop to get a loyalty card?

- Can you invest a few hours of time to do a sample shopping trip and determine which stores have the best prices for items on your list?

- Will you make your lists and analyze which stores will serve your needs best?

4

The Aggressive Discounter

Now that you have seen the benefit of being a non-aggressive discounter, it's time to roll up your sleeves and get to work. This section is for the aggressive discounter who will go that extra mile to save. I am not asking you to alter your taste buds—even though some of you may want to—or to do anything that is unethical. What I am asking you to do is make a plan for discounting. This will constitute taking about an hour a week to formulate a plan to save more money. We will start with the grocery shopping plan that was mentioned in chapter 3. We also will encounter many lists similar to those in chapter 3 to compare the different savings on each item.

You Must Change Your Thinking

Before you seriously start to aggressively discount, you must change your thought process. You must first believe that you are worth saving money for. I say this because you may spend many hours working so someone else can realize his or her dreams but spend little or no time on your own. It is not uncommon for employees to come up with ideas to efficiently help the company they work for, but this same energy is lost when it comes to their own household. I know many people will say that they are more vigilant on their job because this is their livelihood, but what sense does it make to earn a living and squander your hard-earned money? You may spend top dollar for everything even though you can get the same or equivalent things for less money. You must be willing to go that extra mile for yourself.

As a society, we have lost sight of basic principles that once ensured a better life. For example, in ancient times, when a hunter went out to kill food for his family, the hunter killed the animal and did not squander any part of it. The hunter used everything he could from the animal: the hide to make clothes, the flesh for food, and the teeth and bones to make tools. This can be applied to our modern age; examples include people who have a lot less and make their dollar stretch. A homemaker who cuts up a whole chicken and uses the meat for family meals, saves the stock for making soup, and serves the innards to the family dog is doing the same thing—utilizing every part of her purchase. This is what we must do today; we must utilize every avenue to get the most out of our money.

Being called cheap is a form of peer pressure that lingers from childhood because of our innate need to fit in. Ask yourself if the person that's calling you cheap is helping you with anything. Better yet, will they give you what you need when your money runs out because you're trying so hard to live up to their expectations? This goes back to what Momma used to say: "If everyone else jumped off the bridge, would you?"

Use Your Time for Your Benefit

Do you know that your most precious asset is the time that you control? Every time you do something that wastes your time, that time is lost forever. Let's look at it this way: if you work eight hours a day, five days a week, and have an hour of travel time and an hour for preparation, your job takes up about fifty hours a week of your life. Now, if you take into account that you only have 168 hours in a week, you have given almost a third of your week to your job. If you factor in eight hours of sleep, another fifty-six hours a week, you spend a total of 106 hours on work and sleep alone.

You are left with sixty-two hours a week to do with as you see fit. You only have sixty-two hours to develop a more efficient you. You only have sixty-two hours to devote to your dreams and aspirations. You have only sixty-two hours to devote to your church, your family, and any other activity that you enjoy. Therefore, anything that poses a threat to this time should be cut out or minimized. In addition, if you have a second job like many people do, you will have even less time for yourself.

For people with stay-at-home spouses, these figures will vary since the spouse at home presumably shares the workload. For singles that bear the burden of full responsibility for managing a household, these figures may be more accurate. For single parents who have childcare to factor into the equation, they probably have even less free time.

During the workweek, you probably only have about six hours of free time between work and sleep. On your off days, you probably have sixteen hours to do what needs to be done. But let's be honest: during the workweek, you come home tired and feel that you have to cool down from your day at work. Many people do this by watching television or getting something to eat. According to Nielsen Media Research (NMR), Americans watch about four hours and thirty-five minutes of TV each day (NMR 2006).

So, in a week, the average American watches about thirty-two hours of television, leaving only thirty hours to do everything else. With work, television, sleep, and if Internet time is included, there is even less time to do anything else. According to clickz.com, the average American spends over three hours a day on the Internet (McGann 2005). How can you effectively do anything worthwhile with your family or church, do physical exercise, or take time for yourself with these limited hours? For you to get ahead, you must cut out the unnecessary use of your time that will not benefit you spiritually, financially, or emotionally. You have to think differently and use your time efficiently. If you do not value your time, someone else will determine what your time is worth and dictate the direction of your life.

When you work for someone else, they have determined your time to be worth x dollars per hour. It is amazing to think that when it comes to saving money, you may think that your time is too valuable to waste looking for discounts. However, the discounts typically return more money per hour than working most jobs. For example, if ten minutes filling out the discount card application at the grocery store nets you $12 of savings on your first visit alone, then you have effectively made $72 per hour! If clipping coupons for ten minutes saves you $10 on your weekly grocery bill, then you've made the equivalent of $60 per hour. Using this perspective to see that spending time to save some money can really color your attitude toward taking on these new tasks.

Remember, your mother wanted you to be different; she did not want you to be like everyone else. Stop idolizing the few that have not allowed laziness to hinder them, and start utilizing your time to help you get ahead. Get out of the victim mentality, and take charge of your most valuable asset—your time. If you are able to better control your time, you will be better off. If your time does not serve you, then you are a slave to whatever your time is used for. I know your mother did not raise you to be a slave. Remember what your momma would say about doing what everyone else is doing: "If everyone else jumps off the bridge, will you?"

Become a Monthly Grocery Shopper

One important way an aggressive discounter saves money is by becoming a monthly grocery shopper. Ask yourself how many times you have gone out to eat because you did not have enough food at home for a meal? If you make the extra effort to shop monthly instead of weekly, you will save countless dollars every month. I know that there are certain items that will not last the entire month like bread, milk, and eggs. However, many items will last a month. In the end, you will save on gas, time, and the need to pay more for items because you are low every week.

Bulk shopping has always been cheaper than "right now" shopping. If this were not the case, why would bulk-shopping retailers like Sam's Club and Costco, generically called warehouse clubs, be so popular? They know that it is cheaper to buy in bulk per unit, so they can charge their members an annual fee for the privilege. This means that when you shop weekly, you are buying less and paying more per unit. This adds up week to week, month to month, and year to year of you being robbed of your savings. If shopping for "right now" items were cheaper by the unit, do you think Sam's Club and Costco could get away with charging an annual fee? In addition, don't you think there would be a commercial campaign showing that your local stores are cheaper than these bulk stores?

As you get better at discount shopping, you should get a membership at a warehouse club, because there will be times that items you need in bulk will not be on sale at the grocery store. Shopping at these warehouse clubs will save you a considerable amount of money. These warehouse clubs sell more than just food. They also sell clothes, electronics, movies, games, game systems, toys, books, and more. In addition, for the membership fee of about $35 to $50, which is nothing compared to the savings you will receive, you can receive additional discounts for travel, rental cars, hotels, life insurance, prescriptions, and other items.

Most of the grocery items that will not last a month will last at least ten days, so you will only have to shop one extra time a month for a few items instead of four full grocery trips. The extra time that you shop for those perishable items—milk, eggs, fruits, and vegetables come immediately to mind—will probably take you less than thirty minutes.

There will be those that say they don't have time. But why would you make yourself do a job four times when you can do it only once? Put simply, if the average shopping trip is two hours and you do it once a week, then you spend eight hours a month shopping. The time spent shopping for the same items—your staple groceries that will last a month—will take you an additional thirty minutes to an hour for a total of three hours. Your second shopping trip in two weeks to pick up those items that cannot last a month will take you another hour for a total of four hours. In essence, you are trading eight hours a month for four hours a month, giving yourself a discount of 50 percent off your shopping time. By shopping monthly, you are essentially saving yourself four hours a month that can be used to focus on your dreams and ambitions. As an aggressive discounter, you can even discount time!

Comparison Grocery Store Shopping

As an aggressive discounter, you'll also realize that one store does not have the best prices on everything. Many grocery stores sell the same items, but each will price the items differently. That is why an aggressive shopper must comparison shop. My personal suggestion is to comparison shop at least five stores: two large grocery stores, a neighborhood grocery store, and two pharmacies like Walgreen's, CVS, or Rite Aid. You do not have to visit each store, but at least get the sales paper from each of the five stores. For small town areas that only have one of each of these types of stores, you can compare like items from each store and decide for yourself where the best place to make your purchases is.

Also, many of you will utilize bulk-savings stores like Sam's Club and Costco. This is a good idea. These stores are excellent when you need to buy a large quantity of particular items, such as meat, fruit, vegetables, toiletries, cereal, and candy, just to name a few. These stores sell items in large quantity at typically lower prices per unit. Although these stores sell many of the items your local grocer sells, there are various reasons why many of you do not use them: they are not available in your area; you may like to shop at grocery stores; you do not need large quantities of any particular item. So, I will not discuss the bulk-savings stores and will concentrate instead on the type of stores listed earlier.

Therefore, to start your comparison, get the Sunday paper and the weekly food paper in your area. (This varies by metropolitan area; in some places this will be Wednesdays, in others, it's published on Thursdays.) The two pharmacy sales papers are either mailed to your home or are in the Sunday papers. Now that you have all five sales papers, it's time to do a price comparison. We must first designate which one of these stores will be our main store. I suggest you choose one of the large grocery stores because they typically have a bigger selection than the neighborhood store. After selecting your main store, make out a grocery list. Be sure to generate a list that works for your family's situation. While it might be useful to know that Huggies are cheaper at the drugstore than at the grocery store, if you don't have an infant at home, this is useless information. Base your list on your actual consumption. There is a generic list in the appendix that you can add or subtract to as you see fit.

On a separate sheet of paper, write the names of all five stores across the top of the page. Look at your list and then at the sales papers to see which store has the lowest-priced item. Then put the name of the item under the name of the store. Continue to do this until you finish your list. All the items on your list that are not for sale will go under your main grocery store. After you finish this list, I suggest that you go about getting the items from the four other stores and take them home before shopping at your main store. The reason I suggest this is because if you shop at your main store and shop at the other stores, you will have a lot of exposed items in your vehicle. This could lead to your vehicle being broken into, which would spoil the joy of saving.

Alternatively, you could make your list, then window shop and price items at each store. This method requires an investment of time at the outset, but it is time that you only have to spend once. Knowing that diapers are consistently cheaper at the drugstore frees you up from buying them at the grocery store. Conversely, certain items are only available at grocery stores. Your choices for things like fruits and vegetables are more limited.

I did another random shopping experiment during the same period of August 7–13, 2006, but this time I used five different stores to see if the savings were significant to justify going to different locations for groceries. What I will do is use the list from chapter 3 without the loyalty card and the list after using the loyalty card and shopping at the other four locations. Again, to be fair, I included items that were not discounted, no matter the method of purchase.

In addition, to account for the gasoline cost, I will add $6, about two gallons of gas at the time of this publication, to the price of going to the four additional stores. If your car gets twenty miles per gallon, then the $6 will cover forty miles. You will not burn forty miles going to four additional stores. Even though, as a monthly shopper, you would not pay additional for gas because you are not shopping as often. For the sake of this exercise, we will add the $6 to show you that you still will save even adding gas money.

Canned/Jar Foods	No Card/One Store	With Card/Five Stores	Savings
Mushrooms	$1.59	$1.00	$0.59
Peas	$0.75	$0.65	$0.10
Green beans	$0.95	$0.50	$0.45
Corn	$0.95	$0.50	$0.45
Baked beans	$1.69	$1.25	$0.44
Pineapples	$1.52	$1.52	$0
Soup	$0.89	$0.89	$0
Spaghetti sauce	$2.69	$1.25	$1.44
Total	$11.03	$7.56	$3.47

Snacks	No Card/One Store	With Card/Five Stores	Savings
Granola bars	$3.56	$2.00	$1.56
Crackers	$2.19	$0.99	$1.20
Cupcakes	$3.69	$2.50	$1.19
Peanut butter	$2.99	$1.99	$1.00
Strawberry jam	$4.49	$3.99	$0.50
Grape jam	$3.49	$1.00	$2.49
Total	$20.41	$12.47	$7.94

Cereal/Grains	No Card/One Store	With Card/Five Stores	Savings
Spaghetti	$1.29	$0.50	$0.79
Cereal	$3.49	$2.15	$1.34
Bread	$1.29	$1.00	$0.29

Hotdog buns	$1.29	$1.00	$0.29
Hamburger buns	$1.29	$1.00	$0.29
Macaroni	$1.39	$0.50	$0.89
Bagels	$1.89	$1.50	$0.39
Pop Tarts	$1.99	$1.67	$0.32
Rice	$4.49	$4.49	$0
Total	$18.41	$13.81	$4.60

Meat/Seafood	No Card/One Store	With Card/Five Stores	Savings
Ham (lb.)	$4.98	$3.98	$1.00
Chicken breast (lb.)	$5.29	$1.49	$3.80
Chicken wings (lb.)	$2.49	$1.25	$1.24
Drumsticks (lb.)	$1.79	$0.79	$1.00
Hamburger (lb.)	$1.78	$1.19	$0.59
Fish (lb.)	$9.33	$5.99	$3.34
Roast (lb.)	$4.99	$1.77	$3.22
Total	$30.65	$16.46	$14.19

Produce	No Card/One Store	With Card/Five Stores	Savings
Potatoes (5 lb.)	$3.99	$1.50	$2.49
Apples (3 lb.)	$3.29	$1.99	$1.30
Pears (lb.)	$1.79	$1.79	$0
Grapes (lb.)	$1.99	$0.88	$1.11
Bananas (lb.)	$0.49	$0.34	$0.15
Lettuce (head)	$0.99	$0.99	$0
Tomatoes (lb.)	$1.99	$0.99	$1.00

	No Card/One Store	With Card/Five Stores	Savings
Cucumbers	$0.89	$0.50	$0.39
Celery	$1.79	$1.79	$0
Strawberries (lb.)	$2.99	$2.00	$0.99
Carrots (lb.)	$1.99	$1.99	$0
Onions (lb.)	$0.99	$0.99	$0
Total	$23.18	$15.75	$7.43

Beverage	No Card/One Store	With Card/Five Stores	Savings
Soda pop (two liter)	$1.59	$0.89	$0.70
Water (case)	$9.99	$4.49	$5.50
Orange juice (gal.)	$3.59	$1.99	$1.60
Lemonade (gal.)	$3.39	$0.99	$2.40
Fruit punch (gal.)	$3.98	$0.99	$2.99
Total	$22.54	$9.35	$13.19

Dairy	No Card/One Store	With Card/Five Stores	Savings
Eggs (doz.)	$1.25	$0.99	$0.26
Milk (gal.)	$3.29	$1.99	$1.30
Cheese	$2.69	$1.50	$1.19
Yogurt	$0.89	$0.50	$0.39
Margarine	$1.79	$1.00	$0.79
Butter (lb.)	$3.65	$3.65	$0
Cream cheese	$3.99	$3.59	$0.40
Ice cream	$5.29	$2.99	$2.30
Biscuits	$1.26	$1.26	$0

Gasoline	$0.00	$0.00	<$6.00>
Total	$24.10	$17.47	$0.43
Grand Total	**$150.32**	**$92.87**	**$51.45**

You would have saved over 33 percent on your weekly grocery bill, including the extra gas you spent shopping at different stores. You would have saved an additional 9 percent by going to the different stores. Therefore, each week you could save $51.45, which is about $205.80 a month. This is a savings of more than 10 percent of the $2,000 take-home pay you were designated in chapter 3. These savings over a three-year period are about $7,408.80 and an annual savings of $2,469.60. You could save an additional $700 a year by traveling to different stores and using your loyalty card rather than just using your loyalty card.

In addition, if you shopped once a month at a single store without your loyalty card, your monthly bill would be $601.28. Shopping monthly at different stores with your loyalty card would cost you about $377.48. (You will pay for gas once a month.) This will save you about $223.80, which is about 37 percent, saving you an additional 4 percent from shopping weekly. This is about an 11 percent savings of your $2,000 take-home pay designated in chapter 3. These savings over a three-year period are $8,056.80 and $2,685.60 yearly.

Your initial investment of time spent researching prices will take up some of your free hours. But the more time spent up front means less time actually spent shopping later. The payoff will be worth it. Most national chain stores stay open late during the week and are open all weekend. In addition, if you cut out a little of your television time, you might find you have all the time you need for discount shopping and savings.

Consider it another way. Say carefully discounting and shopping at multiple stores takes four hours. If you earn $20 an hour at your job, after taxes, you may take home about $15 per hour. You are earning about $60 for every four hours worked. With an eight-hour workday, you earn about $120 after taxes.

If you become a monthly shopper for four hours a month, you will save about $200 a month for four hours, which is about two days pay. By becoming a monthly shopper, you will get two days pay for four hours. Put in work terms, how many of you would pass up working half a day to be paid for two days? Most of you would take this because you get excited about overtime, which pays time and a half. With this method, you make about four times the pay. Turn your thinking around and see it this way. You're essentially earning money by being careful with your money!

Coupons

For an aggressive discounter, coupons are another way of cutting costs. Coupons are a means of discounting that require a little time and effort but will reward you with significant savings. There are a large variety of items coupons can be used for: groceries, toiletries, sneakers, restaurants, amusement parks, clothes, hotels, rental cars, electronics, and almost any household item. Using coupons can save you a lot of money.

People have many reasons why they refuse to use coupons:

- I'm too busy.

- It's too time consuming.

- What will others think?

- I'm not going to let coupons run my life.

- You really don't save that much.

- I'm not that poor.

However, each time you refuse to use coupons, you are giving away money unnecessarily. It seems as though the excuse that is at the root of all these excuses is "What will others think?" If coupons save you money every month, then why should you care when you use them in front of others? The main thing is that they save you money. Isn't that what it's all about?

Since we have been using groceries for our example, let's continue to do so. Many coupons that you will use come from the Sunday paper. In addition, for those of you who are Internet savvy, you can use the Internet to get even more coupons. For now, we will concentrate on the weekly newspaper coupons. Remember that some grocery stores will double the value of the coupons up to $0.50 on certain days of the week, which means that any coupon valued $0.50 or below will double your savings. (Some stores will double up to a dollar, so make sure to look for these types of sales.)

The average Sunday newspaper with coupons costs $1.50 a week, and its coupons can exceed $150. As an aggressive discounter, you will accumulate a month's worth of coupons before you shop. You'll need to spend $6 a month to get about $600 worth of coupons. Even though you will not use all the coupons, you can save a significant amount that will justify buying the paper.

A little time spent initially to organize a coupon system for yourself will pay off in savings. A small accordion file labeled by coupon category (canned goods, frozen, pet food, etc.) can suffice. Some people prefer to take all their coupons with them to shop, so they can pick and choose depending on what type of sale the store might be having. Others like to make their grocery list and take specific coupons with them. Work out a system that's easy for you to manage.

Imagine that you find about $80 a month in coupon savings that you will use. That is an average savings of $20 a week. Of course, you will have to take the time out to clip the coupons that you will use. It should take you less than an hour a month to clip these coupons. It is important that, as an aggressive discounter, you utilize all of these methods to increase your savings. We will use the example we used earlier of shopping at one store with no loyalty card versus shopping at multiple stores with a loyalty card and coupons. We will assume that you save $20 weekly using coupons, spend $6 for gas, and $1.50 for the paper. Look at how this will affect your weekly grocery savings.

Canned/Jar Foods	No Card/One Store	Card, Five Stores, and Coupons	Savings
Mushrooms	$1.59	$1.00	$0.59
Peas	$0.75	$0.65	$0.10
Green beans	$0.95	$0.50	$0.45
Corn	$0.95	$0.50	$0.45
Baked beans	$1.69	$1.25	$0.44
Pineapples	$1.52	$1.52	$0
Soup	$0.89	$0.89	$0
Spaghetti sauce	$2.69	$1.25	$1.44
Total	$11.03	$7.56	$3.47

Snacks	No Card/One Store	Card, Five Stores, and Coupons	Savings
Granola bars	$3.56	$2.00	$1.56
Crackers	$2.19	$0.99	$1.20
Cupcakes	$3.69	$2.50	$1.19
Peanut butter	$2.99	$1.99	$1.00
Strawberry jam	$4.49	$3.99	$0.50
Grape jam	$3.49	$1.00	$2.49
Total	$20.41	$12.47	$7.94

Cereal/Grains	No Card/One Store	Card, Five Stores, and Coupons	Savings
Spaghetti	$1.29	$0.50	$0.79
Cereal	$3.49	$2.15	$1.34
Bread	$1.29	$1.00	$0.29
Hotdog buns	$1.29	$1.00	$0.29
Hamburger buns	$1.29	$1.00	$0.29

Macaroni	$1.39	$0.50	$0.89
Bagels	$1.89	$1.50	$0.39
Pop Tarts	$1.99	$1.67	$0.32
Rice	$4.49	$4.49	$0
Total	$18.41	$13.81	$4.60

Meat/Seafood	No Card/One Store	Card, Five Stores, and Coupons	Savings
Ham (lb.)	$4.98	$3.98	$1.00
Chicken breast (lb.)	$5.29	$1.49	$3.80
Chicken wings (lb.)	$2.49	$1.25	$1.24
Drumsticks (lb.)	$1.79	$0.79	$1.00
Hamburger (lb.)	$1.78	$1.19	$0.59
Fish (lb.)	$9.33	$5.99	$3.34
Roast (lb.)	$4.99	$1.77	$3.22
Total	$30.65	$16.46	$14.19

Produce	No Card/One Store	Card, Five Stores, and Coupons	Savings
Potatoes (5 lb.)	$3.99	$1.50	$2.49
Apples (3 lb.)	$3.29	$1.99	$1.30
Pears (lb.)	$1.79	$1.79	$0
Grapes (lb.)	$1.99	$0.88	$1.11
Bananas (lb.)	$0.49	$0.34	$0.15
Lettuce (head)	$0.99	$0.99	$0
Tomatoes (lb.)	$1.99	$0.99	$1.00
Cucumbers	$0.89	$0.50	$0.39
Celery	$1.79	$1.79	$0

Strawberries (lb.)	$2.99	$2.00	$0.99
Carrots (lb.)	$1.99	$1.99	$0
Onions (lb.)	$0.99	$0.99	$0
Total	$23.18	$15.75	$7.43

Beverage	No Card/One Store	Card, Five Stores, and Coupons	Savings
Soda pop (two liter)	$1.59	$0.89	$0.70
Water (case)	$9.99	$4.49	$5.50
Orange juice (gal.)	$3.59	$1.99	$1.60
Lemonade (gal.)	$3.39	$0.99	$2.40
Fruit punch (gal.)	$3.98	$0.99	$2.99
Total	$22.54	$9.35	$13.19

Dairy	No Card/One Store	Card, Five Stores, and Coupons	Savings
Eggs (doz.)	$1.25	$0.99	$0.26
Milk (gal.)	$3.29	$1.99	$1.30
Cheese	$2.69	$1.50	$1.19
Yogurt	$0.89	$0.50	$0.39
Margarine	$1.79	$1.00	$0.79
Butter (lb.)	$3.65	$3.65	$0
Cream cheese	$3.99	$3.59	$0.40
Ice cream	$5.29	$2.99	$2.30
Biscuits	$1.26	$1.26	$0
Coupons	$0.00	$0.00	$20.00
Gasoline	$0.00	$0.00	<$6.00>

Newspaper	$0.00	$0.00	<$1.50>
Total	$24.10	$17.47	$19.13
Grand Total	**$150.32**	**$92.87**	**$69.95**

Using coupons, you would have cut $18.50 from the $98.87 bill, even with the $6.00 for gas. Your new monthly total for groceries when using coupons would be $309.48. (Remember, you will not pay for gas for four weeks, because you'll only be going once a month.) Your monthly savings will be $291.80, about 14.6 percent of a $2,000 take-home pay. Your savings is about 49 percent when shopping at more than one store with a loyalty card and coupons.

Over a three-year period, your savings will be $10,504.80, which is about $3,501.60 a year. How many people could use an extra $300 a month without sacrificing the products they normally buy?

If we related this to a workday, using the earlier example, it would take about two and a half days to earn that $300. However, you are only using five hours to make what you would in two and a half days of work. Again, five hours for two and a half days of work! This is why we must decide to be different and start using coupons. If you do not, you will forfeit a significant amount of money. Isn't discounting wonderful?

There have been many examples in the media showing individuals who use coupons and pay next to nothing for groceries. In 2004, ABC's *Good Morning America* featured "The Coupon Mom" who bought nearly $120 worth of groceries for under $40 (ABC News 2004)! Imagine getting to the point where you can get your food nearly free. Sounds good, doesn't it? To get to that point, you must practice and learn—through trial and error—some of the secrets of the trade. Therefore, it could be worth $500 a month in savings to use loyalty cards, multiple stores, and coupons.

In addition, there are discount stores as well. For example, Family Dollar and Dollar General, which are associated with great savings, allow the use of coupons on their already discounted prices. Also, many of the store brand products offer great savings, and some taste the same as the national brand product. Store-specific coupons can often be used at their competitors' establishments; you have to ask. Also, a coupon in combination with a buy-one-get-one-free sale provides extra savings. It's a matter of knowing what you buy and knowing where to buy it.

Entertainment Book

There are wants and needs besides groceries that we'd like to get discounted. One very powerful way to get these savings is the Entertainment Book, which gives you a loyalty card as well as hundreds of coupons. This coupon book ranges in price from $25 to $45 and is available in specialized state and major city editions. This book provides savings on restaurant meals, shoes, clothing, airfare, car rentals, movies, sporting events, groceries, and hotels just to name a few.

There are many deals in this book that will save you up to 50 percent on things you already purchase. For example, if you are taking a date out for dinner at Mario's for Italian food, your entertainment card will allow you to buy one dinner entrée and get the other one free up to $20. If you order a $20 meal and she orders a $22 meal, you would only pay $22 plus tax instead of $42 plus tax. That alone is worth nearly the cost of the book.

In addition, there are coupons to get free games of bowling, miniature golf, movies, and other fun activities. Let's imagine that you paid $45 for the Entertainment Book (it costs about $25 in Michigan), and that you and your spouse go out regularly with another couple, rotating who pays for the major outing for the evening. Each couple is responsible for their own food for the evening. Let's say that it is your turn to pay, and you have $120 to pay for the event and your dinner afterward. In addition, you previously agreed to go to a Detroit Pistons game because all of you are basketball fans.

You thumb through your Entertainment Book and locate Pistons coupons that will give you two free tickets when you buy two tickets for $19 to $40 each. You spend $80 for four seats instead of $160 because you have the Entertainment Book. In addition, you can go to Mario's and use your Entertainment Book loyalty card to get two meals for the price of one. Your total savings will be $100, as shown below:

Item	Without coupons	With coupons	Savings
Pistons ticket	$40	$40	$0
Pistons ticket	$40	$40	$0
Pistons ticket	$40	Free	$40
Pistons ticket	$40	Free	$40
Mario's meal	$20	$20	$0
Mario's meal	$20	Free	$20
Total	$200	$100	$100

The book has already paid for itself in one night.

You can also use the Entertainment Book when you travel. Let's say you want to visit relatives that live in the South. Imagine that your family of four is traveling from Detroit to visit your relatives in Birmingham, Alabama. You decide to fly round-trip and rent a car. You do not have to worry about a place to stay, because you will stay with relatives who will also feed you.

You thumb through your Entertainment Book and notice that you have coupons that will give you a discount on round-trip airline tickets. Also, you find a coupon from Enterprise that gives you 20 percent off a rental car. Once you make your reservations, you'll enjoy the following savings from your Entertainment Book:

Item	Without coupons	With coupons	Savings
Airfare	$341.70	$291.70	$50.00
Airfare	$341.70	$291.70	$50.00
Airfare	$341.70	$291.70	$50.00
Airfare	$341.70	$291.70	$50.00
Car rental	$187.00	$149.60	$37.40
Total	$1,553.80	$1,316.40	$237.40

As you can see, you can save a significant amount of money with the Entertainment Book. You saved $50 per plane ticket and $39.40 for your weekly car rental for a total savings of $237.40. That is a savings of over 15 percent. With these savings you could buy five Entertainment Books.

In addition, you can register your entertainment loyalty card online at www.entertainment.com to get more coupons and savings. Whenever you are going to take a trip, you can go online and type in the state, city, or zip code of your destination and get coupons that are specific to that area. You can save wherever you decide to go by just taking a few minutes to register your loyalty card. Moreover, if you have certain coupons in the Entertainment Book that you like, but there is not enough of a particular coupon, you may be able to get that same coupon off the Internet.

I think the Entertainment Book is worth its weight in gold. It provides you with so many distinct savings that you will save many times over the price you paid for the book. If you enjoy these items and activities, you may as well do them for less. Of course, there may be some coupons that you don't use, so you might consider trading with a friend or coworker for coupons you can use. Maybe you don't play golf, but your vegetarian coworker does and will trade you his Outback coupons for your golfing coupons.

Some highlights in the book include a whole section dedicated to golfers and coupons for investors in the stock market for www. sharebuilder.com. There are several places you can get the book: www.entertainment.com, credit unions, schools through fundraisers, Costco, the Sunday newspaper coupon section, or you can call 1-866-592-5991.

Discounted Internet Service

In order to be more successful at discounting and using coupons, accessing the Internet will open a new world. You can save a lot without the Internet, but you can save even more with it. To access the deals, you need to get online. Let's discuss how to get the Internet at a low cost. If you do not own a computer, you can use your local library to access the Internet for free.

For those of you that do have a computer, you can access the Internet for free for twenty hours a month from a dial-up connection through www.netzero.com and www.juno.com. Each of these services provides you with ten hours free each month. There may be a lot of ads and pop-ups, but this should not matter since you are getting it free. If you see ads and pop-ups, click them off and continue to surf the Internet. If you already have the Internet and use it for less than twenty hours a month, you can go to those Web sites, download the programs to your computer, and sign up for the free service. If you do not already have the Internet, you can go to Best Buy, get a free Netzero or Juno disk, and load it to your computer. Think about it: free Internet service that can help you with your discounting. If you feel that twenty hours a month is not enough, then you can sign up for unlimited service through www.netzero.com or www.juno.com and pay only $9.95 a month, which will also keep you free from ads and pop-ups.

Having the Internet will be useful because some companies give exclusive deals to Internet users. For instance, when you rent cars, stay at hotels, or buy airline tickets, their lowest prices are listed on the Internet. If you include the discount you get from the Entertainment Book, you are talking about significant savings.

In addition, many companies urge you to pay your bills online, which save you time, checks, stamps, envelopes, and running to the mailbox. You can set up bill payment through most companies at their Web sites, and your bills will be paid automatically from your bank account often with no extra charge. You can do your banking online at anytime. This helps you avoid traffic, long lines, and aggravation. Remember, to make sure to ask your bank if they charge a fee for this service because some banks will charge you.

There is great concern these days about identity theft. However, using secure Web sites and being cautious about your personal information will help protect you. Legitimate companies use encryption, Web sites with security features, and other methods to protect their customer's information.

Internet Coupons

Internet coupons are the wave of the future. Many Web sites have printable coupons that can be used at restaurants, grocery stores, drug stores, and other retailers. These coupons can be used at some of the most popular stores. For example, the businesses that put coupons in the Sunday paper or in Smart Source dispensers (the red coupon machines in the aisles) at the grocery store offer more coupons online at www. smartsource.com. Even your local newspaper's Web site may offer printable grocery coupons. Check your news stations and other companies Web sites for other details. For instance, the Detroit NBC affiliate provides you with coupon savings at www.clickondetroit.com. Get surfing and save some money with those Internet coupons.

Although Internet coupons are a valuable resource, a manager at Rite Aid told me that retailers have had problems with fraudulent online coupons, for example, people print them out and doctor the coupons, so some stores will not take them anymore. Call your retailer ahead of time and ask if they still take online coupons before you print them out.

Rebates

Rebates have gotten a bad name, but they can be a big help. Some people get upset that the savings on a particular item are not immediate, and they therefore resent the idea of a rebate. However, think of rebates as delayed savings that you have to work for. Rebates give you an opportunity to get items that are expensive for a lower cost. For example, if it takes you fifteen minutes to do the work (filling out the form, making copies, mailing) for a $50 rebate, then you have effectively earned $200 an hour. Isn't that worth doing in the long run? You can decide for yourself which rebates to take advantage of.

In 2004, my wife and I needed a computer because our CD drive was damaged. We waited until the day after Thanksgiving sale, commonly known as Black Friday, to get our computer because we did not want to spend a lot of money for it. The regular price of the computer was $599.99 before tax. But one particular store gave us a rebate opportunity that cut the price to $199.99 before taxes. We had to pay the regular price with sales tax and mail off the items that were required to get the rebate. Six weeks later, we had a check for $400 and a new computer because we exhibited some patience. As an aggressive discounter, patience will become your strength, and that will increase your savings.

Around the same time, a friend of mine also needed a computer. It was the end of August, and my friend's computer went down. My friend used it mainly for Internet surfing and occasional word processing. I told my friend to wait until the day after Thanksgiving sale; we both could have gotten a computer for the same price. He did not want to wait and did not want to send off a rebate and just about called the rebate a fraud. My friend rushed out and bought a computer for about $1,100 before taxes at a retail store. It included the monitor, computer tower, printer, CD burner, and a DVD burner. My $199.99 system had the same specs, except for the printer and DVD burner.

On the surface, it seems that my friend's computer cost more because it had a free printer and DVD burner. However, a DVD burner and a printer would not have cost me $900. Adding these two features would have cost me about $200 more than what I spent. So, I would have spent $399.99 plus tax after the rebate, as opposed to $1,100 plus tax for a computer with the same features. I saved $700 by waiting three months, so patience won out again. I could have understood if my friend depended on his computer for his income or needed it for school at a critical time. However, this was not the case. Therefore, my friend lost out on $700 because he acted rashly and did not have the patience to wait. By the way, I typed this book on the same computer I bought in 2004. My friend's computer went out on him a year and half after he bought it.

You also can get rebates on small ticket items for your household, such as blank CDs, food, clothing, and other items. There are so many ways to find items that you regularly buy that have rebates available.

Some companies allow you to use your computer to apply for your rebate online. I have seen rebates at grocery stores, drug stores, electronic stores, and department stores, so make sure to look at those sales papers to find those rebates. In addition, as you get savvier with shopping, you may be able to use a coupon on items that also have a rebate. There have been occasions where I have actually made money by buying products with coupons and rebates.

Prescriptions

There are ways to save on your prescription drug costs. Many stores give coupons for gift cards when you transfer prescriptions to their store. There are coupons that are worth as much as $25 for a transferred prescription. In addition, many places will accept competitors' coupons, so you can use the coupons at other locations as well.

If you have insurance and your co-pay is higher than $25, you may think it's not worth it to transfer your prescriptions. However, if your prescription has a $40 co-pay and you transfer it to a grocery store, you can use the $25 gift card to cut down your grocery bill. This will make your prescription cost you $15. This is because the $25 was given back to you in the form of a gift card or certificate. If you do not use the coupon, you will be out of $40.

If you don't have prescription drug insurance coverage, you may be eligible for discount programs like TRX Access cards. These are cards that offer a substantial discount on brand name and generic drugs. Also, membership groups like AAA and AARP offer prescription drug savings. Some drug companies, like Bristol-Meyer Squibb, offer their own discount programs for those who can't afford their medicines.

School Supplies

School supplies can cost an arm and a leg if you buy them at the wrong time or the wrong location. For parents with school-age children, buying your children's school supplies during the late summer will garner you big savings. I used the same method as I did with the grocery shopping, traveling to more than one store, but this sale happens once a year and not month to month like grocery shopping. These savings occurs in the middle to the latter part of July, so you must watch those sales papers.

Let's say you have three children and you buy thirty one-subject note-books, six ten packs of pens, six ten packs of pencils, nine packs of loose leaf paper, thirty folders, and six three-ring binders. This table shows the differences in price depending on when you buy these items.

Item	Regular Price Total	Sale Price Total	Savings
Thirty notebooks	$0.99 $29.70	$0.10 $3.00	$26.70
Six ten pack pens	$1.99 $11.94	$0.10 $0.60	$11.34
Six ten pack pencils	$0.99 $5.94	$0.01 $0.06	$5.88
Nine packs paper	$0.99 $8.91	$0.19 $1.71	$7.20
Six three-ring binders	$4.49 $26.94	$0.25 $1.50	$25.44
Thirty folders	$0.49 $14.70	$0.01 $0.30	$14.40
Gasoline	$0.00	<$6.00>	<$6.00>
Total	$98.13	$13.17	$84.96

As you can see, buying school supplies at the wrong time can hurt you. If you waited until July, used the sales papers, and traveled to multiple stores as an aggressive discounter would, you would save almost $85 on school supplies, which is about 86.6 percent savings. I included the cost of two gallons of gas to illustrate that there is no justification to not take advantage of these savings. Remember, the main thing is that you saved a significant amount of money on items that you know you need for you and your family.

College students can use the same savings techniques. You should never buy your supplies from the college bookstore because many items are marked up significantly. For example, I remember a five-subject notebook being sold at a college bookstore for about $6 and at retail stores for $3. Therefore, if you need ten notebooks a year, you'll spend an extra $30 at the college bookstore.

Clothing

Keeping children in line with current fashion can be expensive and gut wrenching. Whether you have children of your own or are buying for nieces, nephews, grandchildren, or friends' kids, clothes can be an expensive proposition. Buying shoes that cost over $100 and clothes that are priced even higher can put a real dent in your pocketbook. It is one of the most heartbreaking positions to be in. You don't want your children to follow the crowd, but you don't want them to be ostracized. Therefore, these suggestions will help curb the cost of spending for your children's clothes and shoes.

First, do not shop at the mall, because the mall has higher prices because of their rental fees. They know you are there for the convenience, so they will not negotiate. Start shopping at outlet stores and discount stores, such as A.J. Wright, TJ Maxx, Value City, Forman Mills, and Burlington Coat Factory. I strongly suggest outlet stores because they sell the same things as the stores in the mall, but you'll get a 20 percent to 60 percent discount. In addition, some outlets do not charge sales tax.

For example, if you spend about $1,500 at the mall on clothes and shoes per school year for your children, shopping at the outlet stores and receiving at least 20 percent off the same items will save you $300. Many discounts will exceed 20 percent, so you can expect more savings by going to the outlet stores.

Now, there are some items you buy, like school uniforms, socks, underwear, undershirts, and coats that are hugely discounted at the discount stores. These stores are primarily located near the mall—some are actually inside the mall—and provide you with a discount upward of 70 percent on many items. It will pay to shop around to save money for you and your family. In addition, www.ebay.com and www.amazon.com sell many clothes and shoes for significantly less than the brick-and-mortar stores. You have to account for shipping costs, but it pays to consider these methods of shopping.

Discount Internet Sites

For general discounts on a variety of items, there are a few Web sites that have saved me over 50 percent on retail prices. Some include shipping for free. For example, www.all-ink.com provides savings upward of 70 percent on ink cartridges with free shipping for all orders over $40. Items like DVDs, books, CDs, toys, clothes, shoes, electronics, and video games can be purchased at a significant discount with low-cost or free shipping on www.amazon.com and www.ebay.com. Also, eBay's other Web site, www.half.com, has even better deals on certain items. Half.com also is known for selling college textbooks inexpensively.

Using certain Web sites, particularly www.ebay.com and www.half.com, an aggressive discounter can gain more savings by buying items used. For example, if the used video games, DVDs, CDs, and books you purchase off these sites have no scratches or torn pages, you will get the same result as they did when they were new. I have bought many used items and have not had a problem with them. For example, a DVD I bought recently was $10 brand-new and $0.75 used. I saved 92.5 percent. If breaking the plastic off a new DVD is worth an extra $9.25, feel free to buy it. But if you are an aggressive discounter, you can get a DVD that plays the same, minus the sealed plastic, for much less.

In addition, there are informational Web sites that can save you money. For example, I have used www.gasbuddy.com to find the cheapest local gasoline in my area. I have also used the Web sites of the two largest newspapers in my area, the *Detroit News*, www.detnews.com, and the *Detroit Free Press*, www.freep.com, to read the daily news for free, saving on a weekly subscription. Most major newspapers are available free on the Internet. Many major stores put their weekly sales paper on the Internet as well. You can go to their Web site and see the sales for the week.

AAA, Not Just Tow Trucks

AAA is one of the most recognized names in the automobile insurance industry, but many people do not know that AAA sells some of their services separately. For instance, you can buy auto insurance or you can buy the roadside assistance separately. In Michigan, there are three annual roadside assistance plans that you can buy. The Basic Plan is $48 and covers a hookup to the tow truck and five miles of towing four times a year. I don't recommend this plan because most people don't usually break down only 5 miles from their destination. The next plan costs $56 and is called the Tow Rider (in other states, this is the Basic Plan). It covers a hookup to the tow truck and fifteen miles of towing four times a year. The Plus RV plan costs $75 and covers a hookup to the tow truck and one hundred miles of towing four times a year. I have the Plus RV service because it saves me from having to pay extra to add roadside assistance to my automobile insurance.

However, this is not the only reason that I believe that the AAA card will benefit you. In addition to the towing service, AAA provides you with other benefits that will save you money, including discounts at restaurants, retailers, and hotels, and for rental cars, flowers, and car repair. For instance, let's say that you receive a 10 percent discount with your AAA card, and you spend $1,000 a year on hotels, retail, rental cars, and the like. Your total savings for the year would total $100, which would pay for the card. In addition to these savings, you can receive higher savings on other items such as prescription drugs and amusement parks that will further increase your savings. Moreover, some AAA-recommended auto repair shops will give you reasonably-priced services and an additional discount for being an AAA member. I used my AAA discount when I needed my car and my wife's car repaired, and we saved over 6 percent off their already low prices. You can visit www.AAA.com or call 1-800-222-6424 for more information.

As mentioned before, other membership organizations also offer discounts on goods and services. If you're a member of a credit union, such as Navy Federal, you're eligible for dental discounts. AARP offers its members insurance products, drug discounts, and travel discounts. Teachers often get special discounts at toy and office supply stores. Some companies can get discounted cell phone service for their employees, and discounts to theme parks are common. It doesn't hurt to ask if you're eligible for any of these cost savings.

Don't Be Afraid, Ask

I have met many people that are afraid to ask for a discount when there is none posted. When you are a consumer, you are providing the merchant with what they need in order to stay in business. You must drop the idea that the merchant is doing you a favor by having a particular product. You actually are doing them the favor by shopping at their establishment. Remember, if the merchant does not provide you with the service you desire, you are free to go elsewhere to satisfy whatever need or want you have. Therefore, it should be their privilege to serve and accommodate you—not the other way around.

It doesn't hurt to ask for a discount. We have been conditioned to believe that, if an item is priced at a certain amount, we have to accept this price. Where does it say that you must pay the sticker price for an item just because it is in a store? Or that it is impolite to ask for a better price? On many items, like food, cars, books, and clothes, MSRP on the sticker stands for manufacturer's suggested retail price, which means the retailer can sell it at this price, a lower price, or a higher price, depending on what they choose. Remember, once you pay the price that the merchant has determined you should pay, then your money and your bargaining power are gone forever. For example, I remember I was in a dollar store buying AAA batteries, and as I was paying for them, I mentioned I was a schoolteacher. The cashier told me that if I had mentioned this earlier, I could have saved about $5 off the bill. This may not seem like much, but if you can save money by asking, why not? It is in your best interest to try to talk down the price of the items you are buying. Many retailers also offer senior and student discounts for purchases. If you're eligible, why not take them?

Sometimes I am amazed at how things from our childhood can cripple us as adults. As a teacher, I have had many students who are afraid to ask questions, even when they are a few questions away from understanding a concept. The most common answer I have received from my students over the years about being afraid to ask questions is that they did not want to appear stupid in front of their classmates. This speaks volumes. This will carry over to other aspects of their lives.

Being told to not ask questions while you are young and being made to feel stupid when you do ask questions can have a profound effect on a child when he or she grows older. As Proverbs 22:6 states, "Train up a child in the way he should go; and when he is old, he will not depart from it." This means that the way in which the child is taught will stay with him or her throughout life. The training the child receives comes from more than just their parents or the family of the child, but also those that are around them. It can happen in the home, school, church, and other places that the child frequents.

There are positive ways that a person can be impacted by what they learn. When I was twelve years old, I had my first experience with having a price lowered. My grandfather was buying a suit for my uncle, and as my uncle was trying on the suit, my grandfather started negotiating. I watched and listened as my grandfather talked the merchant down from the original price to a price much lower, and he got the merchant to include the shirt, tie, and alterations. Therefore, my grandfather got a complete suit for my uncle with shirt, tie, and alterations for a price lower than the original asking price of the suit alone. This experience motivated me two years later to negotiate the price of Detroit Pistons championship shorts and matching shirt short set. Following my grandfather's example, through negotiation, I got the items at a lower price, and the merchant paid the sales tax. You can actually bargain sales tax with a lot of merchants that have stores outside of malls and are not national chains.

As an aggressive discounter, it is important to remember your objective when you are shopping. The objective is to discount as many items as you buy to help reduce your costs. If you are able to talk down the price of some of your items, you can use the savings to help pay for the other items that you will be purchasing.

You must also be creative in the way you ask. Some merchants will give you a discount just because of your creativity. For example, I was a senior in high school and noticed that a store had a 10 percent discount for seniors. Now mind you, it did not say senior citizens, it said seniors. So I went in the store picked out the items I wanted and went to the checkout. As the cashier was ringing up my items, I asked for the senior discount. The cashier looked at me strange. I said, "I am a senior in high school, and your sign says 10 percent discount for seniors." The cashier laughed and said she would give me the discount because I was not afraid to ask and because I was creative.

I recently went to a Boston Market restaurant with my wife to get something to eat. I realized I did not have a coupon, and there was no listed discount. As the cashier was ringing up our order, I asked if they gave a discount for AAA. She said no. I asked if there was a discount for being a teacher. She said no again. I got creative and said, "Do you give a visit-your-city discount?" The cashier and her manager laughed and laughed. But then the manager said that since I wanted a discount that bad, she'd give me one and cut our bill by 10 percent. We got what we wanted, and we got it at a lower price.

You can also call all the companies whose services that you use at your home to get a better deal on these items. Just call and say that you want a better deal than what they are giving you. For example, a colleague of mine told me she had three cell phones that cost her a little over $100, so my colleague decided to cancel one of the lines. The cell phone company let her keep the third line free and reduced her bill to almost half of what she was paying because she called. Take a little time to ask for a better rate on your credit cards, cable, phone, cell phone, Internet, and other services. When it comes to your money, it does not hurt to ask. Even if you are only able to save $10 a month, you'll see an extra $120 a year in savings.

Rain checks are another aggressive way of discounting, but in order to get a rain check, you must ask for it. Many stores allow customers to get rain checks on items that are on sale but are not available. A rain check is a way of guaranteeing that you will have the opportunity to buy the item later at the sale price. All you have to do, if you cannot find the item you are looking for, is ask a salesclerk or manager for a rain check on the item. Some stores specifically state that they do not give rain checks for certain items, but it doesn't hurt to ask. After you receive the rain check, leave it in your glove compartment of your car so you will not lose or forget it when you go back to the store. Also, be sure to ask how long the rain check will last, and periodically check to see if the store has received another shipment of what you want.

Finally, you must be sure that when you ask for something you do not make it easy for others to tell you no. For example, I have heard many people say things like, "I can't get this cheaper, can I? You don't have this in, do you? I can't buy more than one at this price, can I?" Statements like these make it easy for someone to tell you no, because you are already telling them it cannot be done. Instead, you should ask in this manner: "I want to pay x dollars for this item. What can you do for me? Where is x item? I can't seem to find it. I want to buy x amount at this price. What can you do for me?" I'm not saying this is perfect, but it is a lot better than those self-defeating questions I have heard over the years. Work on what you are going to say to get a cheaper price.

When you get in the habit of asking for what you want, don't allow irrelevant traditions to stop you. Etiquette has harmed many people and fractured many relationships. It has put many people who are getting married in a bind over what to do as far as wedding gifts. Many people that are getting married in today's time already have lived on their own and have established themselves. Therefore, they do not need towels, sheets, picture frames, and other items. Think about it: if you live on your own and so does your future spouse, don't you think you two will have these items?

Most newlyweds need money, but etiquette states that one should not ask for money. Many studies have concluded that marriages often end over money, but I believe many marriages end over lingering wedding costs. Average costs range from $18,000 to $27,000 according the Association for Wedding Professionals (Willis 2005).

For example, I know an individual that decided that on his wedding invitations to put "monetary gifts preferred" to let everyone know that he and his wife needed money instead of other gifts. Under much scrutiny, he still put it on the invitation, even though it did not meet the etiquette standard of others. He and his wife received a few traditional gifts, which they appreciated, but the rest were monetary gifts. They were able to pay off some of their credit cards, and the wedding cost did not hurt them at all. They actually came out ahead. Now imagine if the husband had not asked for money and received unnecessary gifts. They would have had to get rid of things and still had all of their credit cards and wedding bills looking at them after the wedding instead of relaxing and depositing the checks they received from the wedding. Which would you prefer?

Singles setting up households can use the same technique; either ask directly for what is needed or let guests make cash donations. Housewarming parties can be both a lovely party and an opportunity to really utilize what well wishers might want to provide.

We must question where these traditions came from to see if they still apply. For example, the average age at first marriage has moved steadily upward since the 1950s according to the U.S. Census Bureau (Kreider 2005). It made sense, in previous years, to buy all the towels, toasters, and items needed for a home, because many couples were just starting out. But in today's society, it's not uncommon to hear of someone getting married for the first time well into his or her thirties or forties. Do you think that most of these individuals did not accumulate, between the both of them, just about all the household products they needed? If your answer is yes, and I believe it is, why give them a gift that is appropriate for someone just starting out as opposed to someone that has already accumulated these items? If you already have accumulated the traditional wedding gifts, why not try to get something else you need. Just think about it.

Get Others to Help You

When I say get others to help you, I am not telling you to do anything deceitful or underhanded. I am just saying that there is a way that you can get others to help you save as you go on this journey. For people who celebrate Christmas, the holiday season is the perfect time to get others to help you save. Many of us receive gifts that we never use and that take up space. We all know that most people agonize over what they are going to get each other during the Christmas holiday. Therefore, I advise you to ask your friends, relatives, and whoever else buys you Christmas gifts to get these specific cost-saving gifts. Each one of these gifts will not cost over $50.

For example, you can ask someone to get you an Entertainment Book, gift cards to your favorite restaurants, a one-year subscription to the Sunday newspaper (for the coupons), a Costco membership, a Sam's Club membership, or similar items. These gifts are the tools that I have told you to use to save you money. If others give you the items, you will not have to buy them yourself. You will be happy because you did not have to purchase these items yourself, and the person that bought you the gift will be happy, because they were able to give you something you really wanted.

Some of you may feel that this is wrong to ask others for specific Christmas gifts instead of letting them choose what they want to give you. I am not telling you to get upset if they don't get the items you requested—accept them joyfully. I am saying why put yourself in the awkward position of explaining why you have not used the Christmas gift someone gave you five years ago. We all have something people have given us that goes unused each year, and we don't want to get rid of it because it will hurt the person's feelings. This is why if you tell others what you want, and it's not that expensive, then you both would be happy because you are able to use what was bought for you.

It is a great benefit to get others to help you save. It not only helps you, but it also helps the people that are buying you gifts, because they will not have to struggle with what to get you. In addition, you will benefit because you will not have to feel guilty that you did not use a particular gift that was given to you. This is a win-win situation for the both of you.

In fact, my wife and I one Christmas requested that we be given gift cards to our favorite restaurants. We were met with a few strange looks and people being surprised at our request. However, gift cards rolled in. For the next year, we seldom paid for a night out. We were able to save the money that would have been spent going out for other things. We were able to enjoy our gifts together and not have the dreaded task of telling people who gave us gifts that we have not used their gift yet. (We also used coupons at these restaurants for even greater savings.)

You've Read It, Now Do It

You have spent the time reading how to become an aggressive discounter. Now is the time to put to practice what you have learned. Although many of these methods are used in specific situations, you can theoretically use them in other situations as well. In essence, many of these techniques are not restricted to one area. By reducing your costs, you will be able to save for you and your family's future. If you continue to aggressively save, you will be able to better prepare for tomorrow and beyond.

Consider the "baby steps" method for learning to discount. Start with making comprehensive shopping lists, and work your way toward being a monthly grocery shopper. Schedule your comparison-shopping trip, making note of the items your family uses regularly. Start a coupon file, and determine if name brand items with a coupon discount are a better buy for you than generic products. If you enjoy restaurant meals and the entertainment deals offered, buy an Entertainment Book for your metropolitan area. Use the Internet for additional savings. Ask merchants for discounts when you shop. When you need a specific item, ask friends and family for that item as a gift.

"God is not a man, that he should lie; neither the son of man, that he should repent: hath he said, and shall he not do it? Or hath he spoken, and shall he not make it good?" (Numbers 23:19)

Things to think about:

- Can you develop a spending plan that incorporates the savings strategies discussed in this chapter?

- Are you willing to shop at a variety of stores and use coupons, along with loyalty cards, for discounts?

- Can you sit down and work up a monthly grocery list that will enable you to do your major shopping just once a month?

- Can you put together a coupon system that will let you use them wisely in order to get the savings they offer?

- Will you explore rain checks, rebates, and other discount methods to help yourself?

5

You Got the Money, Now What?

After implementing the strategies in this book and those of your own, you will save a significant amount of money. Some of you will not fully feel the abundance you have created because you were operating at a deficit, but now you are breaking even or getting a little ahead. Some of you have noticed that you have an extra $200, $300, $400, $500, or more at your disposal, because you have followed these principles. This is a joyous time, but it also can be a dangerous time as well. If you do not know what to do with the money you are saving, you run the risk of blowing it instead of getting the full benefit of it. It is time to discuss what to do with these savings.

Track Your Savings

The first thing you should do is keep track of your savings. Write it down, put it on a computer, and just make sure you have it somewhere where you note how much money you are saving. Consider making a chart and posting it in a prominent place in your home, maybe your refrigerator door or on the wall in your home office. This is important because this will make a good visual representation of how much money you are accumulating. This will let you know if there are areas where you need to make improvements. If you have a visual representation, there is no doubt that you will continue to save. In addition, this will help you to not waste this money. After all, you need to designate what to do with these savings.

Goals

It is important that you set goals for the money you save each month. If you do not set goals or prioritize, you will squander the money you saved. Know what you are striving for. It may be that you want to make a down payment for a house, to fully fund a retirement account, to have a college fund for your children, or to retire early. The list can go on and on, but if you don't plan for your goals, you will not reach them. You've probably heard the saying, "If you fail to plan, you plan to fail." This is the perfect example of this.

For example, let's say that we have two people, Brenda and Linda, who have an extra $800 a month after discounting. Brenda does not have any particular goal, so she uses the money to buy things that satisfy a particular want at that time. In four years, Brenda will have many possessions that will not have much value. When she comes to herself, she will say what most people say all the time, "Where did all my money go?"

Linda has a goal to set aside $300 a month for retirement and save the rest in her personal account. After four years, Linda will have invested $14,400, before interest, for retirement. Also, Linda will have $24,000 in her personal account. After four years, Linda will have a nice nest egg, and if a crisis hits, she will be prepared. However, Brenda, who has no goals, has nothing to protect her in case a crisis arises. There was no point of Brenda saving and blowing her money.

It is important to set concrete goals or plans. Vague statements such as, "I want a new house" or "I want a new car" aren't helpful. By doing this, you are not properly preparing to distinguish what you want. Try breaking down the big goal into smaller sections. For example, if you want to save up a down payment for a house, you might a realistic goal of saving $400 a month for two years. With interest, you'll have about $10,000 in two years. Your goals could range from saving $10,000 to buying a used car or from saving $100,000 for a child's college education to saving $500,000 in your IRA. It could include investing, career, and marriage, because if you do not know exactly what you want, you will settle for what is presented.

You must take the time to set the goals you want to accomplish. You may want to put a time frame on these goals, so you can monitor your progress as you draw closer to that deadline. I am not saying that you must forsake everything else to reach this goal, but giving yourself a concrete timeline helps to draw your focus to the task. Please do not set too many goals because if you are scattered in many different directions, you will not accomplish anything and get frustrated.

Go, pray, ask God for direction, and write down the goals you have and try to achieve them according to the Lord's will. As the Bible says,

"Trust in the Lord with all thine heart and lean not to thine own understanding. In all thy ways acknowledge him and he shall direct thy paths."
(Proverbs 3:5–6)

Consult God, and let him lead you to the goals that are for your life.

Save for a Rainy Day

After you have set a concrete goal, it is important that you set up a bank or credit union account to put aside at least six to twelve months worth of expense money. It is important that you put away this money just in case a crisis comes. In addition, this will give you a nice cushion if you ever decide you need to leave your job or are laid off. In essence, this will be your readily accessible security blanket if times get tough. This money should be easily accessible and not in CDs, savings bonds, or another form that will restrict when you can access it.

Also, this money should only be touched in an emergency. Let me clarify what an emergency is not: birthdays, Christmas, annual vacations, and things you feel you deserve. Here are a few examples of emergencies: money for an operation your insurance will not cover; no income coming in and bills that need to be paid; your only car breaks down and it needs major repair. Emergencies are unforeseen things that come up in life that must be dealt with. If you do not distinguish what an emergency is, you will probably end up broke with no savings in sight and live paycheck to paycheck. So save to provide for what may happen tomorrow, whether it is good or otherwise.

Give to the Lord

What I am about to tell you is the true element of increasing your health, wealth, and protection by doing one simple thing: give to God through tithes, offerings, and giving to the poor, because he is the source that provides all good things and increases them. Don't get me wrong; this is not a prosperity message, but what God promised in his word.

"Bring ye all the tithes into the storehouse, that there may be meat in mine house, and prove me now herewith, saith the Lord of hosts, if I will not open up the windows of heaven, and pour you out a blessing, that there shall not be room enough to receive it." (Malachi 3:10)

This could be wealth, health, spiritual health, or peace that the Lord will provide us when we follow his principles of giving to him. Ask yourself what sense would it make for you to gain all this money and financial security just to drop dead from health issues or some type of attack upon your person. We need God to help us in everything we do. Therefore, we need to do things that God honors.

Save for Retirement

Many people do not have a good understanding about retirement because until recently, most of the people we grew up with had pension plans instead of 401(k) plans. It is up to each individual to plan for retirement and make sure the money lasts. We all have seen older people working at fast-food places or heard of others eating dog food because they could not afford anything else. Remember that survey by the Vanguard Group reporting that 35 percent of older Americans continued work, whether full- or part-time, in their sixties. You don't want to be one of them! By 2017, Social Security, in its present form, will start running cash deficits (Palmer and Saving 2007). Social Security may not be there for the many Americans who plan to retire in the next twenty or so years.

If your employer provides you access to a 401(k) plan, take advantage of the opportunity the government has given you to invest your money before taxes. If you don't have this available, a traditional IRA is also a way to save money pretax. You should consider using a financial planner who can explain to you how to set up your retirement account and what to invest in. Do not be intimidated by the financial jargon these professionals may use. Ask questions about anything you do not understand, and remember these planners work for you. If you don't get involved, I suggest you take a long hard look at the senior citizens working at fast-food restaurants—you may replace them one day.

With the savings you accumulate, you can fund your retirement account. For example, let's say you save $800 a month after all the discounting. Then you can easily put aside $300 a month for your retirement.

There are other benefits to investing in your retirement account, whether a 401(k) or a traditional IRA. You are reducing the amount of income the IRS counts toward your tax bill. If you make $36,000 a year and you put $3,600 in your retirement account, you will only be taxed on $32,400. In addition, the investment in your retirement account will grow tax-free, so you do not have to worry about paying taxes on your gains until you start withdrawing the money during retirement. Now I am not telling you what to invest in—that is between you and your financial advisor—but I am telling you to save for retirement. Talk to your advisors, determine the amount of risk you are willing to take, and continue to monitor what is going on in your retirement account. Your future depends on it.

It is important to consider that you must get guidance from God, set your goals, write your goals down, save for a rainy day, and save for retirement. With these basic elements, you can and will develop into a good steward over the resources God has entrusted to you. You are going to notice steady growth in these areas if you follow God's principles and always pray to him for guidance.

"Every word of God is pure: He is a shield unto them that put their trust in him." (Proverbs 30:5)

Things to think about:

- Consider a visual representation of your savings: a chart, a spreadsheet, or a poster.

- How many months' salary do you have set aside in an emergency account?

- Sit down and establish some financial goals. Do you want to buy a car? A house? Do you want to set aside a certain amount for a retirement fund?

- Will you set aside a percentage of your income for tithing?

6

Preparing the Next Generation

I must implore you to teach the next generation what you have learned. It is your responsibility to inform those younger than yourself of the pitfalls that you have gone through and show them a better way. You probably wish someone had taken you aside while you were younger and showed you a better way of doing things. Just imagine the heartache you could have avoided if you were taught correctly. You must teach out of love, not out of responsibility. The reason why I make that statement is because, as a schoolteacher, I am responsible to teach math lessons, but it is the love shown for the students that makes them want to learn more. It is important to show the next generation how to go about doing things that will save them money and enrich their future.

We need to stop this vicious cycle of feeling that since no one taught us, we should let them learn on their own. In some respects, the younger generation needs to learn some things on their own, but there is nothing wrong with advising them on what they should do. Also, let us not make things gender-specific, as if grocery shopping is for girls and tool shopping is for boys. How do we know if life may not call for each gender to do what is traditionally the role of the other? In essence, I am saying that we should show the younger generation what they may encounter as they grow older.

For example, paying bills, shopping, cooking, and other chores are something both genders need to know to make it on their own. Have the younger generation participate in activities that will show them how to save and negotiate. I remember taking a nephew of mine to a garage sale. The people conducting the sale were selling new and used items. The new items cost at least $15, and the used items cost about $2. The people were selling the items for $5—which was a great savings—but I thought I could get it cheaper, so we left. I talked to my nephew and told him that you never pay full price for anything; always try to talk down the price, but never try to take advantage of anyone. We went back, and I got everything for $4. It really was not about me saving a $1, but it was the fact that my nephew got some knowledge on how to conduct himself when spending money.

I took another nephew to a computer trade show where I noticed a vendor selling math tutorial software. I saw the same software for over $100, but they were selling it for $22. My nephew watched as I talked to the merchant and asked if I could get a discount on the item. The merchant said no. Then I told her I was a teacher, and she gave me a discount of $3 off the merchandise and paid the sales tax. My nephew saw a few things that day: he saw me be turned down for a discount initially; he saw me not give up and try another angle; and he saw me get the discount on the already underpriced product. This is an example of how you can show the next generation that you do not have to take what is presented to you, but you can try for a better result. In addition, my nephew bought an item that normally cost $8 for $1, saving $7 or 87.5 percent. He later told his cousins about his good fortune.

Even if you don't have children of your own, you can reach out to young people you meet through church, scouting, volunteer organizations, and the like.

Take time out and teach the next generation. Teach them to depend on God for his wisdom, and teach them to try to get the most for their money. Take them with you, let them see the transactions, have them help you clip coupons, and have them watch as you search out discounts. The best thing for you to do is let them see and participate with you as you unveil your secrets of saving. Do not use the excuse that since no one taught you, you are not going to help anyone. This is what I call insanity, because if you do the same thing repeatedly and expect different results, you are insane. How can you expect the next generation to progress if you withhold these experiences from them? Look at yourself. Would you truly want someone to go through the trials you have gone through and waste the time digging themselves out of this pitfall in their life? As Proverbs 22:6 states, "Train up a child in the way he should go, and when he is old, he will not depart from it."

Family and Others

After you have realized the effects of discounting and being responsible with your money, you are obligated to share your wisdom with your family, friends, and others. Even if they do not act on the advice that you give, do not get upset with them, and do not hound them. Let them be. If they want your help after you explain things to them, they will come to you. Just tell them, give examples of your savings, and let it alone after that. Eventually, they will realize how well you are doing, and if they need some help, they will contact you. In addition, when they do ask for your help, do not gloat. Be humble, and help them as much as you can. Remember, you are trying to help them get on the right track and not trying to prove yourself right. Therefore, remember to always be willing to help as much as you can.

"Now faith is the substance of things hoped for, the evidence of things not seen." (Hebrews 11:1)
"Train up a child in the way he should go: and when he is old, he will not depart from it." (Proverbs 22:6)

Things to think about:

- Are there children in your life that you can help teach discounting methods?

- Are you willing to show them by example ways to receive good value for their money?

Conclusion

Let us stop fooling ourselves and realize that saving money is what we need to do in order to make it. Prices continue to rise while our paychecks have not, so we cannot live as we once did. We must utilize all the resources we have available to us in order to survive. Live the American dream and not the American nightmare. So, pray, make out your strategy, clip those coupons, get the loyalty card, ask, and discount, discount, discount. Remember, your future can and will depend on.

I ask you to please not let this be another book you read and say, "Good ideas, but I can't do that right now." If you cannot do many of the aggressive discounting techniques, at least get the loyalty card. This will take less than five minutes of your time, but you will still save. As with anything, you will develop your own ways of saving. Once you have a system in place, it will get easier, and the discount savings will multiply. It is important that you stick to what you have picked up in this book and apply it to your life.

Therefore, I thank you for using your most valuable asset, your time, to read my book. I hope that it has enriched your life and your family's. I will end this book by telling you that you are about to become as your mother wanted you to be, unlike the crowd. If you do things differently, you will not jump off the bridge like everyone else. However, if you continue to do the same thing everyone else is doing, this thought might echo in your head when you are sixty and working in a fast-food restaurant: "Momma told me not to jump off the bridge, and I did it anyway."

"So shall my word be that goeth forth out of my mouth: It shall not return to me void, but it shall accomplish that which I please, and it shall prosper in the thing whereto I sent it." (Isaiah 55:11)

About the Author

"It is my belief that people are struggling today because they have not had to be accountable for their choices about money," says Jerome D. Gibson, author of *I'm Keeping My Money*. "It is apparent that people have the attitude that they deserve to have the finer things in life while sacrificing their future and that of their children. People need to realize if they are not careful, they will not have a future, but will become a burden to someone else."

Born and raised in Detroit, Michigan, Jerome was educated in the Detroit Public School system. Jerome received his Bachelor of Science and Bachelor of Arts degrees at Marygrove College, where he graduated with honors and completed a triple major in math, political science, and business marketing. He later received his teacher certification from Marygrove College. Jerome continued his education at Wayne State University, where he received his master's degree in math education.

Jerome has seen a need in the past few years to study and teach others how to master the money that comes into their hands. Jerome believes, "He who controls your time, controls you." This is why he is so adamant about spreading the message to encourage people to take responsibility for choices that they make. It is his ingrained heart of a teacher that makes him want to share simple techniques that will help anyone get closer to their dreams.

Jerome is married and lives in a neighboring suburb of Detroit. He is an active member of Bethlehem Temple Church of Detroit.

APPENDIX
Generic Grocery List

Remember, this generic list is to be used as a guide to help you set up your grocery list. You can add or subtract to this list to help fit your shopping needs.

Canned Foods:		Snacks:	
Mushrooms	___	Granola bars	___
Peas	___	Crackers	___
Green beans	___	Cupcakes	___
Corn	___	Peanut butter	___
Baked beans	___	Strawberry jam	___
Pineapples	___	Grape jam	___
Soup	___		

Cereal/Grains:		Meat/Seafood:	
Spaghetti	___	Ham	___
Cereal	___	Chicken breast	___
Bread	___	Chicken wings	___
Hot dog buns	___	Drumsticks	___
Hamburger buns	___	Hamburger	___
Macaroni	___	Fish	___

Bagels	___	Roast	___
Pop Tarts	___		
Rice	___		
Dairy:		**Beverages:**	
Eggs	___	Soda pop	___
Milk	___	Water	___
Cheese	___	Orange juice	___
Yogurt	___	Lemonade	___
Margarine	___	Fruit punch	___
Butter	___		
Cream cheese	___	**Miscellaneous:**	
Ice cream	___	Spaghetti sauce	___
Biscuits	___		
Produce:			
Potatoes	___	Apples	___
Pears	___	Grapes	___
Bananas	___	Lettuce	___
Tomatoes	___	Cucumbers	___
Strawberries	___	Celery	___
Carrots	___	Onions	___

Reader Resources

This is just a sampling of the many resources available to you for saving money. Many retailers have Web sites where you can sign up for loyalty cards, additional coupon savings, and presale e-mail notification. There are numerous Web sites devoted to using coupons, frugal living, and saving money.

Loyalty Cards:

Barnes & Noble—booksellers
Borders—books, music, movies
Footlocker—athletic clothing, shoes
F.Y.E. (For Your Entertainment)—music, movies, games
Harris Teeter—groceries
Office Depot—office supplies
Winn Dixie—groceries
Kroger—groceries
CVS—pharmacy
Value Center—groceries
Champs—athletic clothing, shoes

Coupons:

www.printcoupons.com
www.toptenlinks.com/cat.php/Shopping:Coupons
www.msnbc.msn.com/id/3076210/—article on how to navigate coupon sites and get the best value for your time.
www.coolsavings.com

www.valupak.com/www.valupage.com
www.smartsource.com
www.ebates.com—rebates, coupon, and cash-back site.

Meals/entertainment discounts:

www.entertainmentbook.com
www.restuarant.com—savings certificates for a variety of local and chain restaurants, organized by zip code.

Other discount sites/programs:

www.trxaccess.com—prescription drug savings program for the non-insured.
www.aaa.com—best known for roadside assistance; membership benefits include numerous travel, car service, and retail discounts.
www.aarp.com—for people over fifty; offers special deals and discounts for members.
www.amazon.com—known for books, Amazon sells a variety of new and used merchandise.
www.ebay.com—the premier online auction and retail site.
www.half.com—partnered with eBay, this site is filled with nonauction merchandise.

Budget/frugal living:

www.thefrugallife.com—site focused on living within a budget.
www.frugalmom.net—site oriented toward parents and family life on a budget.
www.stretcher.com—dollar-stretching suggestions on this site.

Recommended Reading

Listed below are a few books that have helped me in my journey in keeping my money. These books inspired me to continue on this path of financial responsibility.

Clason, George S. *The Richest Man in Babylon*. New York, NY: New American Library, 2001.

Cohen, Herb. *You Can Negotiate Anything*. Sacramento, CA: Citadel, 2000.

King James Version of the Holy Bible

Kiyoksaki, Robert. *Rich Dad, Poor Dad*. New York, NY: Time-Warner Paperbacks, 2002.

Kyne, Peter B. *The Go-Getter*. 1921. Reprint, New York, NY: Henry Holt & Co, 2005.

Ramsey, Dave. *The Total Money Makeover: A Proven Plan for Financial Fitness*. Nashville, TN: Thomas Nelson, 2007.

Ury, William. *Getting Past No*. New York, NY: Bantam, 1993.

Bibliography

ABC News. "Money-Saving Tips from Coupon Queen." July 21, 2004. http://abcnews.go.com/GMA/PersonalBest/story?id=127688&page=1

Ameriks, J., Ferguson, H.B., Madamba, A. B., and Utkus, S. P. "Six Paths to Retirement." Valley Forge, PA. *Vanguard Group* 26:1–28. https://institutional.vanguard.com/VGApp/iip/Research?Path=PUBRR&File=RetResSixPaths.jsp&FW_Activity=ArticleDetail Activity&FW_Event=articleDetail&IIP_INF=ZZRetResSix-Paths.jsp#

Bosworth, Martin H. "Loyalty Cards: Reward or Threat?" ConsumerAffairs.com. July 11, 2005. http://www.consumeraffairs.com/news04/2005/loyalty_cards.html

Consumer Price Index. Inflation Calculator, 1997–2007. http://www.bls.gov/cpi/#data

Fallon, Jeannine. "Average Monthly Car Payments Falling As Loan Terms Extend to Record Lengths." November 25, 2003. http://www.edmunds.com/help/about/press/100956/article.html

Kreider, Rose M. 2005. Number, Timing, and Duration of Marriages and Divorces: 2001. Current Population Reports, P70-97. U.S. Census Bureau, Washington, DC. February. http://www.census.gov/prod/2005pubs/p70-97.pdf

McGann, Rob. 2005. "Internet Edges Out Family Time More Than TV Time." January 5. http://www.clickz.com/showPage.html?page=3455061

National Association of Insurance Commissioners. 2006. "Average Expenditures for Auto Insurance." http://www.iii.org/media/facts/statsbyissue/auto/

Nielsen Media Research. 2006. "Nielsen Media Research Reports Television's Popularity Is Still Growing: Led by Teen Girls, Americans Continue to Watch at Record Levels; Nielsen Able to Provide More Precise Information Than Ever Before." September 21. http://www.nielsenmedia.com/nc/portal/site/Public/menu-item.55dc65b4a7d5adff3f65936147a062a0/?allRmCB=on&newSearch=yes&vgnextoid=4156527aacccd010VgnVCM100000ac0a26 0aRCRD&searchBox=research

Palmer, John L., Saving, Thomas R. 2007. Social Security Administration. "Status of the Social Security and Medicare Programs: A Summary of the 2007 Annual Reports Social Security and Medicare Boards." April 23.http://www.ssa.gov/OACT/TRSUM/trsummary.html

USDA. 2007. "Weekly Food Cost by Type of Family: 2000 to 2005." www.census.gov/compendia/statab/tables/07s0711.xls

Willis, Gerri. Cutting the Bridal Budget. 2005. 5 Tips: Ways to keep the budget in line while enjoying your special day. New York. CNN/Money. June 3. www.money.cnn.com/2005/06/03/pf/saving/willis_tips/

978-0-595-42387-3
0-595-42387-6

Printed in the United States
102883LV00006B/70-81/A

9 780595 423873